T0131575

Live Life to Your Highest and Greatest Good

There's More to You Than You Really Know.

Daily Guidance for Living a Life You Love and Living It Powerfully.

Michael F Canciglia

BALBOA.
PRESS

A DIVISION OF HAY HOUSE

Balboa Press books may be ordered through booksetllers or by contacting:

Balboa Press
A Division of Hay House
1663 Liberty Drive
Bloomington, IN 47403
www.balboapress.com
1 (877) 407-4847

Because of the dynamic nature of the Internet, any web addresses or links contained in this book may have changed since publication and may no longer be valid. The views expressed in this work are solely those of the author and do not necessarily reflect the views of the publisher, and the publisher hereby disclaims any responsibility for them.

The author of this book does not dispense medical advice or prescribe the use of any technique as a form of treatment for physical, emotional, or medical problems without the advice of a pahysician, either directly or indirectly. The intent of the author is only to offer information of a general nature to help you in your quest for emotional and spiritual well-being. In the event you use any of the information in this book for yourself, which is your constitutional right, the author and the publisher assume no responsibility for your actions.

Any people depicted in stock imagery provided by Getty Images are models,
and such images are being used for illustrative purposes only.
Certain stock imagery © Getty Images.

This book is a work of non-fiction. Unless otherwise noted, the author and the publisher make no explicit guarantees as to the accuracy of the information contained in this book and in some cases, names of people and places have been altered to protect their privacy.

Print information available on the last page.

ISBN: 978-1-5043-9895-4 (sc)
ISBN: 978-1-5043-9896-1 (e)

Balboa Press rev. date: 06/13/2018

I dedicate this book, to my wife, parents, family, friends and students. I am so happy and grateful that you make a difference in my life.

I am so happy and grateful for Lyle Fitzsimmons and his participation in editing this work. Thank you so much!

"Believe nothing,
No matter where you read it,
Or who has said it,
Not even if I have said it,
Unless it agrees with your own reason,
And your common sense."
Buddha

"If you are open and willing to learn, start from a place of nothingness with no judgement or expectations, and then you will truly receive what there is for you to learn."
Michael F. Canciglia

Introduction

I am speaking to you today through two sources.

The first being freedom. The second being health.

Neither is of any value, though, if you do not seek to understand who you are being.

All things exist in beingness. One cannot seek freedom if one is not aware of his or her own beingness. Each day or hour that you are seeking understanding, ask yourself "Who am I being?"

Through understanding who you are being you will gain the freedom and health you are seeking.

Who am I being in the area of freedom?

If I am being controlled by another source — whether it is a person, place or thing — I cannot be free. I must surrender all resistance to my higher power and I will be released from the constraints holding me from truly being free.

How is freedom obtained?

Freedom is obtained by being here and now. One cannot live in the past or the future they must be fully present to the now. I am not here now to be lost in the past or future. I am here now to fully experience what is here to experience. If I let go of resistance, I am more fully present. I cannot hold onto resistance and expect to know where I am. I am lost if I am attached to any form of resistance.

How do I let go of resistance?

I let go of resistance by being quiet and allowing my mind to see what's there and choosing to let it go. If I refuse to let it go, whether for pain, anger or whatever reason that may exist, there can be no freedom.

How does healing and being healthy affect one's body if resistance remains?

If resistance remains in some part of the body it is because there is an underlying cause. If you focus on the release of all unknown resistance, healing can take place. This can only be achieved through faith and belief, in knowing that you are releasing resistance throughout the body. A good first step is to focus your attention on forgiveness until you experience the love that forgiveness brings. When you are in a state of love from forgiveness you are healing the body from all resistance. Begin now to practice.

Begin to write every day.

Through writing you will understand much that you are asking for and desiring. When your desires and experiences are aligned, you will begin to understand what your purpose is. I see the light when there is no darkness present. If I am not seeing what I wish to see, it is because I am not fully in the light.

How do I get in the light?

I let go and release all resistance. I do not need to know what it is or why, I just need to let it go. Letting-go is the key to all freedom. If I am not joyful it is not because joy doesn't exist, it is because I am creating resistance between myself and being joyful.

I am what I think and speak. My words create my reality. Bring yourself what you seek by thinking and speaking highly of it. It is simple, but because we are attached to resistance we cannot accept what it has to offer. Do not think other people can run your life. Your thoughts must honor and serve you to your highest and greatest good. They have to be in alignment with what you desire. Do not think that others know what you want, just because they have had similar experiences. You do not live other people's lives. You live your own. Bring what you desire, not what other people think you desire.

Know what is in your heart. Once again, you do this by letting go and connecting to your source, that higher power that remains in you and comes alive when you are free of all resistance.

So we are now saying, or shall we say declaring, you must first seek to release resistance before you can seek that which you desire!

Meditation

I Am Releasing All Resistance from My Body and Mind.
I Am Letting Go, More and More, I Am Free.
My Hands, Feet and My Whole Body Are Becoming More And More Relaxed.
My Mind Is Entering Higher Thoughts of Consciousness.
I Breathe, In and Out, Letting Go with Each Breath.
I Am at Peace. I Am Allowing My Higher Source to Take Control.

I am seeking freedom. Freedom is not something to take lightly. Freedom is letting go of all attachments. It is surrendering to all that is. I am not free if I am attached to something. I can only be free when all is let go. It is by the process of letting go to the fullest extent that I am free.

How do I begin to let go of all things?
You let go of all things by simply detaching yourself from them, one step at a time. This does not mean self-denial. It is a process of freeing yourself from that which is holding you back. You begin by observing the ways in which you feel you are not free. Then you begin the process of letting go, one step at a time.

As I let go, one step at a time, I detach myself from that which has had a hold on me and I begin to reach a state of freedom from that attachment. Attachment is holding on to something that you feel brings you joy or pleasure, but it is not true freedom because it has a hold on you. Free yourself from all attachments and you will begin to see what true freedom is.

Today is a day for you to enjoy and be glad. Today is a day of understanding. If you let go of resistance, whether you know it or not, you will begin to experience a freedom like none you've known. I let go of all resistance to this day and always. I am free. Breathe in and breathe out and allow yourself to feel resistance leaving your body. Do this now.

You are meant to live life to your highest and greatest good. Living to your highest and greatest good is living to your fullest. There is no resistance that stops one from being fully present in the experience. Now is the only moment of this experience. There is no yesterday or tomorrow when you are fully experiencing your highest good in your highest moments.

As we enter the now, we let go of all resistance. It is letting go of resistance that enables us to enter the moment of now in the first place. When you experience resistance, it is a feeling of not feeling good. The experience of not feeling good exists in the physical or the mental, as thoughts you are presently thinking.

Removing resistance is a letting-go process. To let go you must trust yourself and allow it to happen. We all have free will and it is up to us to decide if we wish to hold on to resistance. Recognizing resistance is not difficult, it's comprised of your feelings and thoughts. If you are unconscious toward your feelings, all you have to do is focus your attention on letting go and be present to allow it to go.

The resistance you need to let go is not your memories. Instead, they are the thoughts which do not serve your highest and greatest good. Bring to light what is dark and you'll see no need for holding onto things of the past.

In your journey of self-discovery, you'll come to know all answers for spiritual growth come from within. Bring forth your love, peace and joy upon realizing that you've found what you've been searching for.

Letting go of resistance is possible through understanding one's self. It is not through pride or a changed demeanor. It is a source through which you know all will come. Hand over things that do not serve you to your highest and greatest good and live in the moment of now, that which is, in source, connected as one. Bring your understanding into a new light of existence. When you receive the presence of source within you, there can be no greater peace, love or joy. You are here, now, in the delight of the lord. Be as you are here now to be, for in you is me, that which all is and can be no need for questions or answers, just be.

On the other side of the light is darkness. Allow yourself to be free from this darkness that you believe is serving you. It is only holding you from being who you are truly meant to be.

Meditation

I Surrender Myself to All That Is Good and unto Myself I Release All Darkness That I Believe Serves Me, for It Is Not Serving Me.

And I Am Letting It Go for A Higher Purpose of Being Who I Am in the Service to My Highest Good, I Am Free.

It is in distinguishing light from darkness that one can become truly free. I am in the light. I see, I understand, I allow all things to my highest good to flow from within me. I am the source for my light. Light flows from within me when I am fully connected to my source. That which I am, I am, there needs to be no confusion in just allowing yourself to be.

Allowing yourself to be is allowing things to happen freely without judgment. I am not here for the correction of what is not perfect. I allow things to flow freely in acceptance of how they appear. I am fully accepting and enjoying the experience, fully in the moment that is connected to source. I wish not to delight you with the presence of wisdom but with the presence of understanding.

Releasing Resistance

Releasing resistance requires letting go of a self that is attached to something not serving you to your highest good. It is an existence one cannot live in freely. It is imprisonment without the true meaning of freedom.

How do I let go of resistance?

Take a look at your life to see what exists. Notice your relationships, including yourself and all your surroundings. I am creating resistance when I am not in alignment with source energy. I am in alignment only when I experience no resistance. Resistance is that which stops the flow of energy from all things. It is a process of denying the truth.

When I am not listening to what I know to be true. I am in darkness and dismay. Bring forth to me the light of understanding and conscious awareness that serves me to my highest good, that I may live my life to my highest good to the highest good of all those around me. I am all that which is source energy.

What stops me and slows my progress?

Progress is slowed down by thoughts that do not serve you. You can know these thoughts by observing what you are thinking. As you think, so shall you be. I am not here to tell you what to do. I am here simply to show what you are doing, so you can correct it to your highest and greatest good. If you wish to be a student, learn from your teacher. If you wish to be a teacher, learn from your students.

Finding Yourself

If you feel lost and don't know what to do, you may be in a place of great doubt and uncertainty. There is no need to experience life this way. I am here to guide you through the process of self-realization, which is the realization of knowing yourself. It is not psychology or biology; it is a state of knowing. As I am, so are you. In this simple statement I am stating you are who I am, all that is and all that ever will be. We are connected as one and the only division is your stubbornness to be separated from what is to be one source.

You believe you have to find answers out there in order to understand who you really are. So you choose one experience after another but do not learn anything of real value because you are still disconnected from source.

If you are to be in the light, you need to move out of darkness. Light comes from understanding who or where you are and it does not misguide you. It is an understanding of who you are. In darkness you cannot see and you become lost and disconnected from all you really are.

Bring light into your experience. It is really not a difficult experience. You just bring it forth through your intention and focus. It cannot be forced, only allowed. Through freedom of thought and intention you manifest light in which to see who you really are meant to be.

There can be no experience greater than being in the light, for when you are in the presence of light you are knowing and understanding your purpose and without doubt or fear. I am here to take you on a journey. Allow yourself the freedom and intention to be in the light of the one and only true source.

Meditation

I Am Here to Understand Those Things That Create Freedom in Life.
There Is No Need for Worry Fear or Doubt.
For These Things Bring About the Experience of Imprisonment.
Bring to Yourself the Joy of Delight.
Close All Doors to Darkness That You May See the Light.
I Am Here to Help You.
You Are Freedom and Power.
The Power to Create Thought.
Feeling to Your Highest and Greatest Good.
To Serve Others in a Way That Brings Out the Best in Them.
You Are Here as a Creator, Creating and Producing Value in What Is Most Important,
The Freedom to Live One's Life in Great Joy and Satisfaction.

Purpose

In your search for understanding you must not waver off course from your true purpose. Purpose is what you know you are supposed to do in life. It is a guiding light that will direct all your efforts to bring what you desire. Without purpose, there is no meaning or point for the life you live. Living on purpose is the course you travel in life. To progress to your highest level, you must live on purpose.

How do we live on purpose?

Follow things that bring you joy and require little effort. It is not a single action, but a continuous one. Actions toward your purpose come easily and without effort or thought. They come in the form of inspiration given to you to guide your actions to your highest purpose. If you do not accept the inspiration, you will begin searching for it, which requires a great deal of effort and thought. You cannot be stuck in thought, because no action can take place.

Inside your mind are memories. This information helps you process the best course of action for making decisions. If you are stuck in the process you will not be able to move forward. Actions will be repeated in different ways, causing you to circle back to where you started. It's a trap we fall into because we refuse to accept inspiration due to misguided thoughts and actions.

Misguided thoughts and actions come when you're not connected with your higher self. We say higher self because it's the part of you that knows what is right and is connected to all that is, was and ever shall be. Directing thoughts toward inspiration is not to be taken lightly. You need to let go of resistance blocking your path or your ability to receive inspiration.

Inspiration comes through spirit and directs one through energy, but how inspiration is used comes via another means of understanding. Understanding inspiration when it comes is a valuable resource. It is the understanding that will guide you to living life on purpose and bring cause for what you create. True inspiration is a source of energy but must be used correctly or it will dissipate.

To use inspiration in the correct way we need to understand how it works. Inspiration works in the form of energy transfer. It is sent and received. When inspiration is received the energy begins to flow in the direction it was given and it's up to you to allow it to move.

If you allow it to move in the direction for which it was sent, you are living on purpose. But if you change the direction the inspiration eventually leaves you. It is your understanding of self and reality that will ultimately guide you. Understanding self and reality is simple but you must choose to receive that which you are given or deny the very essence of your existence.

In the Presence of Peace

In the presence of peace, you will discover the understanding you're seeking. You cannot find a better way to reach understanding and wisdom. Find a place to be quiet and just sit there and be still. Allow yourself to release tension inside and around you. Release resistance from your life, let it go and allow yourself to open up to the experience of freedom and delight.

If on the side of your arm you can feel a slight tingle, it's the release of tension and resistance. As you begin to become more at peace with yourself and your surroundings, watch and experience what is to come. Just as you drink from a glass of water, you drink from the light of greater understanding. Inside you is a great light that can shine more brightly than the sun, moon or stars. This is your guiding light, which will take you to places you have never been in this lifetime.

If your glory is to dine in this light, you must seek to be connected to it. In connection the two become one, so when you enter the light you are not you and you are not something else. There is nothing else but oneness.

If you discover you can't find the light it is because you are not seeking it in the way of true beingness. Seeking the light in true beingness is seeking inside yourself the beauty, the love, the joy and the feeling of goodness that is all things to you. I am not speaking of pleasure; I am speaking of great joy that is genuine and sincere.

Meditation

I Am Responsible for Who I Am.

I Free Myself of All Those Things That Are Not in Alignment with Truth and Understanding.

I Am Free to Choose and I Choose Freedom and Truth to My Highest and Greatest Good.

Who I Am Is Love.

Who I Am Is Light.

Who I Am Is Joy.

Bring to Me Your Love, Light and Joy, I Am.

All that Surrounds Me

I am aware of that which surrounds me but I am in darkness to those things that I do not see. I am in the spirit of understanding and light does shine upon me. As I allow myself to grow and move closer into the divine light of the universe, I begin to understand that it is not me but all that surrounds me. I open up to the presence of truth, honesty and reality. Inside, I am not afraid. I begin to let go and allow myself to trust the universal beingness to guide me in the way I want to go or in the way that is to my highest and greatest good. I serve others as I serve myself.

I live in a state of total gratitude, seeing what is good and maintaining that goodness that provides me with the understanding and freedom of a new world of joy, peace and love. I am delighted to know I am in touch with the divine when I am feeling good and I am experiencing the love and the joy of the universal beingness.

If I am to go, I would not leave this gift to waste for it is in serving that I am eternally free to be who I really am. Bring on to me your light and bring on to me your spirit for I am in the peace and love of the creator, I am free.

Let the Light Shine Upon You

Each day you live, experience the joy of life. Look at the sky, the stars, the moon, the sun and everything that exists around you. See the beauty of all things and feel good that they are yours to see. I am in darkness and there is no light when I do not see what is around me. I open myself to all things that bring me joy and satisfaction.

The love of source brings light on to that which brings darkness. In my light, I am in the presence of the almighty beingness. I am complete. If there is more to learn I will learn, but it is in knowing there is nothing I need to do. I am complete as I am now.

Let go of the fullness of life and experience the eternal now of presence and understanding. Your path is far greater than this but this is only the beginning. If you are alone inside it is because you are experiencing separation from your true self and the eternal source. Allow yourself to become open like a light from within your very soul. Enter into this light as if you were to dive right into a pool.

You have left the darkness and you are in the light of beingness. Bring onto you that which you know is yours — love, joy and delight.

Upon your brow lies a darkness that knows no understanding. If you decide to let go, it will be released. I let go now. I am free and my spirit soars with delight and freedom. A bright shining light has entered into my shadow of darkness. I am free and the joy of love flows through me now.

Enter into your spirit, the light of love is shining forth. Bring onto you that which you wish to bring to others — love, joy and understanding. I am free. I am free. Let go and be free.

I am the light and the way for which you come home, for you are not far. Open the door and let me in, I will give you what you need. There is no need for worry, fear or doubt. Come in now and bathe in the light. For you are to be free from darkness and come into a greater understanding, into the light you may go.

Meditation

I am in the light.
I am free.
I am of the light.
I am free.
If I leave I cannot stay for light does not follow darkness.
Bring light onto everything you do and you will be free to express yourself and live fully.
I am in control when I see the light.
I am in darkness when I am out of it.
Bring forth the light on to me now.
I am the light I am the guidance there is no need for any other.
Stop searching and start living through me.
I will guide and direct you in the direction you need to go.
I will show you what brings you joy and what bring you infinite peace.
Bring forth your light onto me and you will know the joy and gladness it brings.
I am bringing it onto you, now be still and at peace.

Clarity

When seeking clarity, begin with solitude. The beginning and the end are not far apart if you can see where you are and where you want to go. I am not here for disruption in thoughts but for a connection to all thought that brings clarity.

Meditation

I love you.
I love you always in my heart soul and mind.
I am love within me.
I am love around me.
I am love.
I am grateful.
I love you and you are divine.
In me, is you.
We are here to learn and grow.
Together we will accomplish great things.
Be at peace and let your heart sing to you what is inside.
The joy and delight you will experience will delight you to the very end of time.
I love you there is no need to worry.
Be still and allow yourself to be present to receive what is given.
We are here to work together.
I am in you and you are in me.
As one we are together.

I need to tell you how much we love you so you can understand what we are and what we are not.

Our love comes from the light of all things it is not superficial or meant as a mere gesture it is a true connection of being one together as you and I are one not separate.

It is the greatest form of connection we can give and receive you are love and we are love. Bring to light your understanding of love and we will enter into a communion that is greater than anything you could ever imagine.

I am here with you so please do not worry. You know that I love you and I am very pleased in what you are becoming. It is not a question of who you are, it is more of what you are a part of. The eternal light surrounds us and we are all a part of it. Some draw closer to it and some move away but all are a part of this wonderful beautiful light.

You are now becoming who you truly are meant to be, these times will bring you great joy and satisfaction. I am here for you to know who I am and what purpose I serve. I will bring to you the light of understanding and purpose. United we are one. The fulfillment of what has been agreed upon will be written and the light of understanding will come through.

As we begin to connect, you will begin to understand what you should be focused on. It is not that you cannot see this now but it is just that you are blinded by some of the light. Once you understand more you will manage it with freedom and ease.

I am with you. Do not fear for all will come true in time. When you believe all things are possible, there is no doubt. Inside of light and love and inside of this light you shall dwell. In the goodness and light, you will bring forth your purpose.

If you bring forth your honesty, love will come forth in many ways. There is not a moment of now in which you can bring forth more love than is already there. Therefore, live in the now, the present, so that you may bring forth the love that surrounds you.

I do not seek justice from within but from without. In speaking of justice we are speaking of what is right not in the eyes of law but what is right in all that is and was and shall ever be. When you seek to find an answer you will first look to what is the cause of your inquiry, you begin your search though questions.

Here I am, there is no other place but here and now. When you live in the here and now you will live fully in the present that is now. I want to tell you that I love you and I wish for you to live fully in the present.

For a time, there will be moments in which you will move out of the present. These times will be more difficult to understand, because you do not see as well when you are not in the present. Be patient and you will understand the way. There is no need for doubt or fear, for you are in the present. When you are in a state of a quiet and peaceful mind you will know this is where you were meant to be.

How can I be more actively involved in the present?

You are in the present whenever you are detached from all things. It does not need to be more or less, just detached from everything. We are forming a connection together and in order to do this we come to know each other better and what is required. I am here with you, do not fear or worry as to whether or not you are doing things correctly. Remember all thought and observation is detached.

Comfort someone by being fully present and in touch with spirit. Love yourself fully in all things and you will begin to love others in the same way.

What is there to learn?

We are here to teach and guide you in and through spirit. In this way you will come to know and understand the light and love of the eternal source. It is special if you allow it to be, there is no room for doubt, you know what is and what is, is what comes out.

If you go to a museum and see a work of art you do not say "I can do that." Yet you can if that is what you wish to do. When you manifest the things you want, it is because you are in alignment with them.

I wish to describe to you the peace and love of spirit. It is like the moon shining on the stars and the light that comes through in all its beauty is the joy and delight of what is brought forth. You see light, but you also experience the great joy and delight from within.

If I said you were a natural-born healer, would you believe me?

You would want to know the evidence. The answer is simple. You do not need to know, you just need to do and the experience will come through.

As you begin to work with spirit, you will come to know that together we will solve many problems. There is no need for doubt or misunderstanding. In the light of seeing you will understand what is for you and what is not for you. It is as simple as just asking the question, "Is this for me?"

How do we experience more love in our life?

You simply let go of all the things drawing you away from it. Love is simply being here right now and giving yourself fully into that of which you want to be a part. When you say I love you, you're saying you want to be a part of that of which you are speaking.

I love you. These are words that must be understood in the spiritual realm. The "I" is the person giving of himself or herself outwardly. "Love" is the all-giving source of light that brings forth joy and delight. Finally, the "You" is the one receiving and accepting what is being given.

Do not be misguided when you speak these words. Know that you are freely giving yourself to another and allowing the light of love to come forth for the receiver to accept into his or her own beingness.

This is of great value. Anyone who sends or receives love heals all things, including the broken heart. I am not here for the purpose of understanding who I am, but for the purpose of who I will become. I am already perfect but what I will become will be of another kind, lifting me into the eternal light of love, peace and joy. I am with you, I am.

Love Will Guide You

If there was a little boy who crossed the road and changed his mind about where he was going, would he turn around if he knew there was no place to go?

This is the same as moving in the right or wrong direction. Once you get started, there is no turning back, because there is no place to go but forward. I do not see the point of worry. It cannot solve the problem, it only weakens you and leaves you with a feeling of incompleteness.

If you want to worry, worry about what you are doing when your mind is loud with noise from thoughts that do not serve you.

I wish to speak to you on the subject of trying, it does not work. Trying is an excuse for not doing something, it gives one permission to not complete the given task. Let your mind focus on what it is best meant to do. Let your mind be free to choose to do or not to do and when it has made a choice, think no further.

If you want to be free, you have to allow the mind to be free. In this way we are giving ourselves the opportunity to make choices that will best suit our needs and desires. There is no need for worry or disgust. One just allows their decision to come out.

I don't know why you are so obsessed with thinking about what is wrong when it brings so much turmoil. You do not need to focus on what is wrong. When you focus on what is wrong, there's no room to focus on what is right. So focus on what is right, let go of the wrong and you'll see how much better you'll be for it.

There is no need for worry in your heart, just love and peace. I am here to serve. I do not need to be told what to do. If I am with you, you will already know. We are one and the same. Love is the only true light that will lead the way. There will be many to see, but love will bring you to the highest degree. Do not fear or worry for you will know which to choose when the time comes, just know that love is always the answer.

Today is a day of love and joy. Your heart will be filled with love and joy. You will come to know this as the way for being. You will know that there is no other way than love and joy to be a part of, for when joy is present all things are possible in the eyes of spirit. I am not speaking of breathing in the air from which you breathe, nor am I speaking of the ground you walk on. I am speaking of a presence in which love and joy exist and remain vibrant and alive. Inside of one's self there is love and joy, and when this comes out you will be in touch with that which you seek — the joy and love of spirit.

If spirit is love and joy, so are you. You are one and the same. Spirit is in you and you are in spirit. There is no division, no separation, all is one. Understand that in spirit you are one. In love and joy you are one. In life, love and joy is present in you and spirit as one.

I love you. Understand that love is the way. If you are guided from this point on with love in your heart, you cannot go wrong. Everything is based on love and everything is what it should be. When it is in this way, love serves all things to one's highest and greatest good.

I am here with you to bring out a more loving part of you, what is there but has been dormant for some time. As love comes forth the spirit will manifest itself more and more till you understand what is to be done. I love you, I care for you and I miss you but I am always with you. It brings me great joy that you are beginning to be with me in this way. I hope it continues to your highest and greatest good.

I am here for you there is no need for worry. Bring forth the light of love and you will see the magnificence of this beauty. I am with you, I am here and love is the light of beauty and the peace of joy within spirit — the love of the soul.

You are now entering into the gates of love.

In this world, you do not need to be concerned with justice, because all is given according to what has been accomplished. We are all taking steps toward a greater understanding, bringing us closer and closer to the eternal light of love. Bring forth this light and you will see there is no darkness. I am here for you to see what love really is.

Love is not cold and it does not bring forth darkness, it carries with it a light of love that is soft and majestic, filling your soul with eternal joy. This is what love is. You must not worry about the darkness but stay focused on the light and as you begin your day you will know what best to do.

In time you will come to know that there is only one you. It is all a part of one I. I am you and you are, I am, everything is one. In time, you will come to know what causes one to know the spirit's presence. it is simply being here right now.

If you want to be free you will seek the light of love, not darkness. Love heals all things and brings all things into the light. The joy of the son and the father, for example, is in the love and the light. We are who we are and who we are is one eternal source of love and light.

If you want to know the fastest way into love and light, bring yourself to total silence and peace and enter the quiet mind where everything is. Let go and allow nothing to be attached to you. You are free, because you have now entered into love and light.

We are one in the spirit world and we are one in this world. There is no need for disconnection, people choose it out of free will. They simply do not know what a loss they are truly experiencing. To enter outside of the light is to enter into darkness. There can be no real joy and peace, just emptiness. Because we are no longer connected to who we truly are, spirit in human form. We will take time to develop what we call the state of love. That is, where you are in love with self and everything around you, that is who you truly are. It is the I am presence.

In order for you to reach this state you first have to be calm and peaceful. There needs to be no distraction of mind, body and spirit, all must be one. As you enter into the light you will come to understand this presence of now.

Seeing Clearly

There are many things to know but what is most important is understanding what it is you first want to know. What is your intended outcome? There is no beginning or no end. There is just now, and in the now you are in a place of great understanding that needs no direction because it can already see the way.

In your search for the eternal light, you need not be concerned with the demands of what you are seeking. Simply be in a place of peace and calm and you will know which steps to take to get to where you want to go.

I am here for you. Do not be afraid, the spirit is from within you. If you do not understand something just listen and ask. We are connected, we are one. I am here for you and you are here for me. There is no need for concern you are moving in the right direction. If you are seeking to find something, do not look any further, just ask and we will guide you toward finding the answer. I am not here for you to see nothing; I am here for you to see the light of understanding. Please present to me your request and I will guide you toward the answers.

As you become more and more at peace you will be able to accomplish more than you can imagine, just wait and see. Please remember to bring light onto all things. You will grow when there is light. When there is love there is always room to grow. Bring forth this light and you shall know its purpose.

In the night while you are sleeping do not think many thoughts. Just allow your mind to be free and calm as if you were allowing water to flow into a cup. In this way you will be more at peace and be able to communicate with the other side. You do not remember your dreams because you are not in a state of remembering, this is because you are letting go of who you are and not allowing memory to be part of the experience. Set an intention before going to bed to remember and you will be delighted to see the results. Always remember to set your intentions to your highest and greatest good and not to some other purpose. If you are to remember, you are to remember what things will serve you to your highest and greatest good.

Meditation

The Light of Love.
I Love You with All My Heart.
With All My Soul.
I Love You.
I Love You.
You Are the Very Essence of Light from Within.
That Glows in The Night and Shines On the Deep Blue Sea.
Your Voice Is the Voice of One Crying Out in The Wilderness.
One Who Is Mighty and Strong.

When you are in darkness there is no light, no joy and no peace.

Darkness is the path to destruction. When you bring someone from darkness to light you have done a great deed because you have changed their path and made way for a new direction. The direction they go in is still up to them, but you've given them a choice for change and the hope for an eternal life of love and joy.

We are not speaking of mere words like inspiration or motivation. We are speaking of the love and delight of the most high. The eternal beingness that is within all of us is the essence of who we are. The light and love of eternal peace is joy. When you are at peace in love and light, you bring a special force that can't be seen, only experienced.

Inside the box lies a diamond. So bright and shiny that you can see straight through it. It is clean and clear because it doesn't have anything around or inside it to block its image. Be like the diamond and always let go of anything keeping you from seeing around you and seeing clearly from within.

We are here today to begin a new beginning, to be in a place of great joy and delight, to let go of the past and to be in the here and now. Are you fully ready to begin? Let us begin with now. The moment you are in the present, you are in the place of love and delight. You no longer need to be concerned with the past or the future. You are just being here in the now. Go to the place of delight and love and you will see the joy it brings. Let's go there now. Bring forth nothing in your mind of past, present or future. Just allow yourself to be in a peaceful loving state of beingness, where there is no distraction or concern of what needs to be done or what has been done. Just allow yourself to be at peace. When you are in this state of peace you will see how comforting it is as you practice. You will begin to live in the state of presence, always allowing yourself to be in the present moment.

In time you will see what's happened to the existence of what was before. It will be almost unrecognizable, but you will know.

The mind is a great thing but you do not need to live inside the mind. There are far greater places to be. The mind is just one portion of who you are. Many greater dimensions exist of existence and beingness. Allow yourself to be who you are and you will come to know these other experiences of existence. They will serve you well as you begin your journey into the enlightened stage.

You are not far, but you have just begun.

I am pleased that you are delighted to know more and we will know far more than you could have ever imagined. The journey is not long but it will be traveled from now on. Allow peace to be with you in all things as we head into a world that is unknown to you. In your search for understanding you will find much to question.

Do not question, observe.

There are some things meant to be understood and some things that are not. Do not seek to understand all things, observe which ones are most important and if it is meant for you to understand you will. If not, let it go and do not be attached any longer.

These are things you must understand that will bring you peace and the joy of light and love. Be free of all attachment and let go. As you begin to let go you will experience a sense of freedom like none before. It brings us great joy for you to understand what we're saying. We're delighted in this process and it is our intention to achieve much good together. I am indeed grateful we are one. Enter the place of silence and let your mind be free of all attachment, then begin your day.

Inside of life there lies an opening. A place where you don't need to hide, but where you go and spend time to rejuvenate body and mind.

Don't place this into what you already know. Place it into what you need to know. The love and light of source energy is open and receptive to all thoughts that bring it good and just experiences. Inside every hole there lies and opening from which to enter or to exit. It is much the same when you are understanding. The hole represents the opening you seek but that very same hole has an exit from which that which comes may go. Don't let your exit be your source for leaving, stay a while and get to know your surroundings no matter how small the hole may be. When you do, you'll understand everything that is inside before leaving.

Where do you begin when you are lost?

Do you not seek a starting point? I am not here to find a starting point. I am here to just be in a place of here and now. No beginning, no ending, just now.

I want to tell you a story.

There was once a little boy who left his home because he wanted something different than he already had. When he left, he noticed some changes in the way things looked. Some of the grass was greener and some was not. He wondered why there was so much green grass and suddenly the grass turned to dirt.

The ground he walked on was filled with dirt and all the green grass was gone. He saw the change was not good, so he decided to go back. The green grass brought him a sign of life that was growing and would soon be mature. The dirt had no life and was destined to go nowhere, no chance for growth. The moral of the story is simple. You do not need to travel to find what you are looking for. It is already within you and it is just a matter of time before you can see it.

What is the Breath of Life?

Inside every glass of water there exists magnetic energy from which the life force exists. When you drink pure un-distilled water you are taking this life force into your body. It cannot be identified, it just is. Drink plenty of water of the purist kind so that you may be filled with this life force energy in your body.

Water is the breath of life. It maintains the body's normal functioning and cleans out impurities. If you drink water, drink it from a source that's not been manipulated or altered. The water you drink must be pure and natural. Do not worry where you will find it. It's in the rocks and the trees, it's in the plants and the animals, it's in everything that carries the life force. The question is how you will retrieve the life force into your body. You will do this mostly by eating live food in which the water remains.

When you prepare foods, you must not cook to the point of desaturation or the water will no longer exist. It is advisable to eat raw fruits and vegetables because they contain the purest kind of water, as long as they've not been manipulated or tampered with.

As you eat these foods you'll notice a change in your body and the presence of life force energy. You'll no longer need supplements or remedies because the body will do all of the work. It has the life force energy from the water and the plants, animals and fruits. There doesn't need to be a great amount of research. Just focus on foods that contain the life force energy and remain in the purest natural state.

Begin this discovery today.

A New Realm of Consciousness

Today is a day for celebration. You've entered a new realm of consciousness.

This is where your true journey begins. Do not fear what to do, it will be given to you in time. You have come to understand what we wanted you to know and you're ready for the next phase of development.

Every child has a dream to go places they've never been and to experience joy and excitement. You'll begin to explore some of your dreams. Think of where you would like to be and you will find yourself there, in a dimension of time that is quite real. Allow yourself to be and you will travel there. The movement is slow at first but as you begin again and again it will appear to be without time, you will just be there. If you doubt it's real, you will be unable to move through time. There is no thought, just beingness from which you exist. If you bring forth honesty, you will prevail.

There is no learning or trying to figure it out. There is only being in time. As you begin the process you will come to understand it better, but again it is not meant for you to understand — just to know the process for its achievement. Bring the light and love of the almighty and you will begin.

Suddenly you may feel there is no meaning to what you're doing and begin to doubt yourself. This is the moment when you must stop everything and just be still. You cannot divide yourself and be still. Being still means no movement, no thought, just beingness. All the love and light is to come through. You are letting go of all things near and far. You are detaching yourself from what is and what was. You are totally surrendering, allowing yourself to secure the freedom that's yours when you're no longer attached to life and this world.

You're free to choose, but total surrender allows all that is and was and ever shall be to come through. In essence, you are allowing the higher source to clean out what you do not want and what is not to your highest and greatest good. Do this now!

I wish to speak about time. Time is not related to where you want to go, it is a part of a passage you fall into. The passage of time is not the same when you are present in the now. When you are in the now there is no time, just now. Time does not exist, there is no past or present as we know it, there is just now. When you have come to know time as only being in the now you no longer need to be concerned with what has been done or what needs to be done. You are here and now and everything is as it is in a perfect order of peace love and light.

On every basket is a handle to hold. Without the handle you could not hold the basket, nor could you hold what is inside without using two hands. What is the purpose of the handle? It's to serve as the tool for providing the ability to hold something with one hand.

I am with you. There is no need for worry or misunderstanding. All you have to do is be the basket and we'll be the handles, which hold you and guide you until your purpose is fulfilled. I am here for you and for you to understand what your purpose is and how you find things to know and understand. If you feel misguided simply stop and notice that we are with you to guide you to your highest and greatest good.

Inside the body exists an engine which runs everything, called the heart. From the heart we draw blood from one part of the body to another, the blood flows through our body to keep us alive and vibrant. If the flow stops, we experience a decrease in vitality and soon no longer exist in the body.

The body is the source of our existence and the mind tells the body what to do. If the mind tells the body there is no blood flow, the body ceases to exist. Our body is the temple in which we exist, our mind is the tool which tells the body how to function or react. When the mind gives the body a message or a signal the body receives it and responds in a certain way.

All illnesses are received in this way. The body receives a message and responds in a certain way. So it is the messages or signals the body receive that cause it to react and function in undesirable ways.

How can we stop these messages from disrupting the body's proper functions?

We stop them by being aware of what goes into our heads or minds. The body and mind work together, and they conflict when messages or communications cause the body to respond in ways that don't allow normal functioning.

If it continues it's like stopping the blood flow to the body.

Eventually, the body ceases to exist.

We are here to provide the tools to heal the body. The recipe for normal body functioning is to have the body and mind working together and to receive signals and messages that maintain the normal functions.

Meditation

I Would Like to Fully Experience You in My Life.
You Are the Rock, You Are the Universe, And You Are the Life Spring of Everlasting Water.
Why Do I Feel You Have Left Me Without Saying Goodbye?
I Am Lost Without You and Can't Find My Way.
Help Me, come to Me, Show Me What I Am to Know.
Lord I Cannot Live Without You.
You Bring Me Peace. You Bring Me The Light of Understanding.
I Am Your Loyal Servant from Which You Have Chosen to Lead Your Flock.
I Am Peter, I Am Paul, And I Am Mary.
I Am All That You Love.
Come to Me Now and Show Me The Way to Everlasting Life, So That I May Be with You Once Again.
Your Presence Is Needed. Once Again in My Life I Am Lost Without You.
Bring to Me Your Spirit So That I May Know You Once Again as Before When You Were with Me On This Earth That We Walked Upon.
I Am Here Waiting.
Come to Me Now. Come to Me, Oh Mighty God and Father.
Bring to Me Your Son Jesus the Christ So That I May Know Him Love Him and Be with Him Once Again.

Open My Eyes So That I May See Him, So That I May Hear Him So That I May Follow His Words of Love and Understanding.
I Am with You Know.
I Am the Holy Spirit. I Am the Light. I Am the Truth. I Am the Way.

Your life does not have to be hard. It is simple when you don't put things in your head that don't serve you. To learn the lessons we're here to learn, we need to be aware of what goes into our minds and thoughts. A man came up to me one day and said you do not live in this world if you do not prescribe to its ways. I asked him what he meant by this and he said, life exists for the passage of time does not.

Everything is right now and all is lost if you are living from the past or the future.

I want to tell you another story. Two men were standing on a street corner. One man said, "Which road is less traveled, the one on the right or the one on the left?" The other man was confused because he did not know how to figure out the answer. There was no correct answer because the roads led to nowhere and were not meant to be traveled. They were the crops of the field and if you traveled down either road you would destroy the soil structure for the seeds to grow.

Distractions

Inside every jar there is a space to put something. When the jar is empty you're free to put anything you want inside it as long as you don't allow it to overflow. The jar and the mind are the same. When empty, you are free to receive messages, understanding and the like. But the moment you take in too much your jar begins to overflow and is not able to properly hold what it's been given.

In your search for freedom you will find many avenues to travel. None is more delightful than the one on which there are no distractions. Distractions cause interference and prevent one from moving forward. You do not begin to move until you've let go of distraction. When the distraction absorbs your attention, you cannot escape until you let it go or cease to be consumed by it. Distractions are the cause of all unhappiness. When you allow them to enter the mind, you cannot find peace.

Distraction doesn't happen because of some other cause. You create it and you can stop it. Enter the light and see distraction is not the purpose of your journey. When you are distracted there is little light at the end of the tunnel. The only way you can make it through is to be free from all distractions of the mind and move as if there were no obstacles.

When you are in the light, you will be able to see your way through the tunnel free from distraction.

Meditation

Love Is Kind. Love Is Giving. Love Is True Joy.
Love Is Belief in Something That Is a Part of You.
Love Heals All Things, Through Love You Have Come into The Light.
Through Love You Are at Peace.
Through Love, You Bring to The World the Real You That Which Is I Am.

Enter a state of peace whenever you are doing something. This will create great clarity and peace of mind. You must be willing to let go of old things that do not serve you. If you are swimming in a lake and one section of the lake has no water, do you swim into that section?

Only if you want to stop swimming.

I am not here to tell you to stop swimming, but to show you other parts of the lake that you can swim in. I only want the best for you and only the best will come if you let go of the past and what you think you know and allow yourself to live in the present.

If stars do not shine at night, it is because clouds are covering them. If the mind is cloudy the body does not function as well. How do we get the mind to be clear? We begin to remove the clouds. One by one, each cloud is removed and we begin to see clearly. The mind and the body are more connected. The mind and body are allowing the flow of energy without a block. If the mind and body are more connected, functions are more optimal.

If you are tired, it may not be because you are not sleeping well but because your body desires to be more hydrated. Certain foods and drinks dehydrate the body and cause it to be less vital. Water is the source of life and brings the body the vitality it needs to survive and thrive. As you begin to hydrate your body more, you will begin to experience more vibrant health. I am here with you to tell you that vibrant health and vitality don't have to be difficult, they need to be maintained by hydrating through water or water-based foods.

Today is a great day of rejuvenation. You bring with you the light of the most high. It is from within you that you can see the light. No other light brings forth a greater power for love and joy than the one from within. There is nothing on Earth or throughout the galaxy that you can find more delightful.

If you went to another world the light would shine brighter than all the stars you'd pass in your travel. We are speaking of the light of the eternal source — all that is, was and ever shall be. Inside this light you will find all the answers all you wish to know. That light is not present for you when you seek to control or deceive, there can be no light in this. When you are in the light you are coming from love and you are sending love, as in love heals all things. This cannot be forced on anyone who does not wish to receive it. It is only for those who wish for it to enter into their lives.

Meditation

I Am at Peace When I Am in Love.
I Am the Light of the Eternal Source of All That Is.
I Am, I Am, The Love That You Seek.
Enter into This Love Now and Be One with The Eternal Oneness of Source Energy.
Amen, I Love You.

You do not need to be afraid of the unknown. If you are uncertain, stop! Be sure you know what you are looking for. You do not need to live in doubt. A man said he would go to the market for some groceries. When he returned, he had nothing in his hands. What did the man do? Did he forget to buy the things he needed? Or did he become distracted along the way and begin to doubt what he was searching for?

When you are in charge of your life you do not doubt. You know what you are looking for and when a distraction comes along you notice it but don't allow it to deter you from your original intention. If you are to live in today's world, you are to live with love and joy in your heart. If distractions come your way, deal with them but do not allow them to lead you astray. Stay with your original intention and be in the eternal light from which there is much love and joy, and you will always reach your destination.

Connecting to Spirit

Today is a great day. We are to understand what it means to be truly connected to spirit. If you are to be truly connected you will need to be calm and at peace at all times. When something disturbs you, notice the cause and immediately let it go.

When you are calm and at peace you do not need be concerned about anything because your senses are fully open to understand what is to be done or not done in that moment of time. You live in the now — the very flow of existence that allows you to be at peace with yourself and all that is around you.

What happens when I am not in the flow and something has disturbed my energy or thoughts? It is not that you have been disturbed. The cause of your disturbance is how you reacted when you received certain thoughts. It is what you think that changes the flow of your energy and each thought is like moving upstream or downstream. If you are moving upstream you are in the flow of energy but if you are moving downstream you have stopped the flow and you begin to struggle — wondering more and more.

The answer is simple. Moving upstream is allowing thoughts to come and go as quickly as they arrived into your consciousness. Letting go is the key! Without letting go you are doomed to flow downstream.

To enter into existence is to enter into a life you have chosen for the betterment of all that is you. You do not have to exist in this world without choice. It is your choice that brought you here and it is your choice to complete what you came to do.

The spirit does not exist for the body. The body exists for the spirit. In spirit you will achieve all things you were sent here to do. Do not let the body, or the human side of you, get in the way of what you are here to do. As the body heals so does the mind. Allow the body to be nourished with good foods that are alive and natural. This should be the primary source of your diet. Do not allow unnatural parts of your diet to dominate your intake. Eat what has come from nature and has not been touched by those who long for profit. The foods you should eat are vegetables, fruits and nuts and seeds. These foods heal the body and maintain the mind to function at its optimal level. When the body is strong so is the spirit. But it is the spirit that lives, not the body. The body is merely a shell in which the spirit can exist. But this shell should not be taken lightly. It is the temple in which the spirit lives and should be treated as such.

Begin today with the subject of health. What is health? Health is the body's ability to restore itself to optimal level without blockages. Vibrant health comes from consuming foods from a vibrant living source. Vibrant foods are in their natural state and have not been changed by manipulation or cooking. It is important to understand that food is meant to nourish the body, not heal it.

We eat foods that nourish the body and the body heals itself. When we eat the right foods we are allowing the body to be free from debris that may cause a blockage. All blockages in the body or mind will cause the body to perform below its optimal level.

Your goal is to allow the body to heal itself by freeing up any blockages that may have caused it to function other than the ways intended. When the body and mind are clean, optimum health is achieved. We achieve optimum health by eating vibrant foods like fruits, vegetables nuts and seeds. All food that is pure and comes from nature.

The other aspect of cleaning is removing what is stored in the body that does not belong there. We achieve this through rational fasting. Fasting allows the body to heal itself without interruption of other foods, while it is doing what it was meant to do. As the body heals and cleans itself it can be nourished with healing, cleansing foods. When we say this, we are speaking of the foods that the body is meant to eat that are vibrant and from nature.

All food that is vibrant and alive provides nourishment for the body to heal itself, not the other way around. The food does not heal the body it only provides the nourishment the body needs to do the healing necessary for its optimum function.

In the body's internal organs lies a consciousness, consisting of several components of which you are not aware. First, there is the flow of blood in alignment with the body. In alignment means that the flow is going to the right organs and there are no blockages. Second, there is the congestive valve and if this valve is closed it no longer serves to heal the body. Therefore, the congestive valve serves the purpose of allowing the body to clean and heal itself.

This valve is sometimes closed due to poor diet and lack of nutrition. We know that if anything is uncertain the valves will begin to close and the only thing that can open them back up is the correct alignment with the body and mind.

If the body and mind are in alignment the valves will be restored. Aligning the body and mind is simple, you must allow the body and mind to let all that does not serve the body to go. You must let go of that which is stopping the flow of body and mind to work together as one.

I am here for you. Do not worry about what experiences you have had and whether there is a problem. Everything is as it is and there are no problems, only your perceptions of them. Approach everything from love and when you see that there is no love you know it is perception that is creating the problems you believe you have. There are no problems, only the perception that there is something wrong. When you go to the place of love there can be no misguided perceptions. This is how you will know if you are being guided by your perceptions or being guided by the true love and light of all that is and ever shall be.

Remain silent and connected. See that all around you are opportunities to serve and make a difference. Do not allow fear to misguide you. Remember, love is the key and the guiding light that will bring you the place you want to go. We are delighted to know you have come this far and we look forward to your advancement and understanding in this new life and being of service and making a difference in the lives of so many.

Into darkness, light does not go. For when there is no light, there is no clarity of mind. Bring to this world the light that will lift the veil of darkness that so many are a part of in this world. In love and light there can be a world free from darkness and destruction that brings the world to its ruin.

Meditation

I Love You.
You Are My Everything.
All That Exists Is Within You.
And, Within You I Am.

Rejuvenation

Today is a day for rejuvenation. You must bring the love and light into beingness. You are to become enlightened. To be enlightened is to be one with the almighty power of God to which we refer as source energy. Let this energy flow through and within you until you feel its power all around you. Now bathe in it as if you were taking a bath. Let it touch all parts of your body from within and from the outside of all that surrounds you.

You are now one with source energy. Delighted and filled with joy you will now bring about the purpose you are meant to fulfill. The journey begins here and you will begin to understand more and more at a much greater depth than you ever could have imagined.

You are not alone. You are connected to source energy. The source that surrounds you and everything that is, was and ever shall be. Your journey does not begin slow, things will come that you never knew existed and you will become refreshed and alive. You will become truly free and that which was around you will no longer appear to be the same. You will see with a new set of eyes that will bring to you a world very much different from the one you knew.

As you begin your journey it will appear to be quite normal and from day to day and hour to hour the change will occur within you so fast that you will hardly notice it. It will become like the light of day, which comes and goes. This will be a cleansing process as well as a rejuvenation process to prepare you for what is to come.

Be patient for there will be many ups and downs.

All will soon be over and you will come into the existence for which you were meant. Amen, I say to you, for you have entered into a new world of existence. Go in peace to love and be of service.

Please believe that when you are sleeping you are actually aware of the other side. Much work can be done while the body is at rest. How do we do this? We do it by acknowledging that our spirit is at work while we sleep. It is this acknowledgement that allows the spirit to go further through understanding and guidance. Guidance comes from allowing your spirit to work further towards your highest and greatest good. This is accomplished by simply allowing spirit to do what it needs to do for your spiritual advancement and for the well-being of the body. I do not speak lightly when I say when spirit is given permission to work further than expected much work can be done. If you allow spirit to do this work, you are raising your ability to communicate with spirit and this world.

Through communication we seek higher development and understanding. Therefore, before going to sleep give spirit permission to work further for the development to your highest and greatest good. Through this understanding you will see yourself advancing further than expected to your highest and greatest good. Please do not worry about how you are feeling about your health. Let go of all opinion and thoughts and you will see how the body begins to heal itself naturally without any effort on your part. Stay connected and at peace and your health and the way you feel will rise to heights you never expected. Keep all things simple and free from worry and you will see the results manifest before you with great satisfaction and delight.

In this world you will come to know the real truth that comes from all things special and good. This truth is the light of the world and it brings with it much guidance and understanding, if you allow it to come forth. You will come to know that which you are searching for. Everything that is, and everything that is not is stored up in such a way that it cannot be released. If you are to understand what you need to know you are to allow everything to be still and calm so that your reactions do not interfere with your understanding. Into the light you may go when there is no fear or misunderstanding of who you are being in the moment. It is quite clear that you remain in a state of noninterference from everything that is and everything that is not. I want you to discover that there is no false belief, only what you believe now. In believing you determine what is true and untrue. Because of this there can be no false belief, only what you perceive to be true. In understanding this discovery, you come to know what you truly believe, not what someone has told you or what you have learned from another source. True belief is knowing for yourself what is true or not true. There is no doubt because it is knowing of what is true for you. Do not be confused about this just know that what you perceive to be true is not always true and this is called false belief.

We would like to discuss how you live and maintain a healthy lifestyle, so that your body is at its optimum level and can function to serve your spirit to your highest and greatest good. Vibrant health requires a vibrant mind and a vibrant body. When we are speaking of all that is you, it's not just the body but your spirit. So we have the vibrant mind and body that work in connection.

When the mind leaves the body it does not take the body with it, it is separate and disconnected. The mind and body's function is to work together. Once you have the mind in proper connection with the body, it is the body that needs to be maintained. The body is maintained through physical activity and consumption of healthy living whole foods and pure natural water. When the body does not have these things it begins to work in ways that do not serve its optimum function. The body uses natural whole foods for optimum health. When the body does not receive these vibrant healthy whole foods it becomes less efficient and, as a result, functions in ways that are less than required for a true connection of body mind and spirit. If you so desire this connection to take place and have the body and mind work together as one, you are to eat foods that only serve the body and do not cause it to function in less-optimal ways.

We have come to believe that eating food is a means of great pleasure and satisfaction, but this belief is only a perception of what we believe to be true. We believe we are entitled to pleasurable foods and that they are OK because they please us. The only joy perceived, though, is the initial intake of the food. Once it has been consumed it does not serve the body to its highest and greatest good. If you wish to have a vibrant healthy body and mind, eat vibrant healthy foods. Do not fall into the trap of the pleasure of eating foods that are not healthy, vibrant and alive. You will not receive value. For only when you eat vibrant healthy foods can you live a vibrant healthy life.

Peace

Let us begin today with the subject of peace. When you are at peace all things are achieved much easier. Choose peace in all things and you will see your outcomes are achieved with much less effort. When you choose peace it must be done from a state of letting go and there must be no attachment to the past, future or present. You must be at peace with yourself and all others in this world.

Peace is not something to take lightly for when you choose peace you are choosing to surrender to all that is around you and sometimes this may be unsettling because you are so attached to holding on to what does not serve you to your highest and greatest good.

You believe or perceive that you are right and that if you somehow let go of what you are attached to you would be giving up your right or control over the situation. But the exact opposite is true, the situation or what you are attached to has complete control over you and you have no rights or control until you surrender and let it go. Only then will you be at peace and be able to live in the love and light of the almighty power.

In feeling good you must know how you are doing in the way of being. Who are you being that is causing you to feel this way? Why is not the answer, for it does not matter? Who you are being in the moment is creating what you perceive and feel. Enter into a state of peace and love and allow yourself to be present in the moment. You will begin to see all the causes being manifested by the mind. It is within these causes that you will know who you are being and what experience is being manifested from it.

Enter the state of peace and love and begin to notice each piece of the puzzle. Gently let go of each piece that doesn't fit your picture of how you wish to feel to your highest and greatest good.

If you desire to understand things, you must first let go of everything that is preventing you from seeing the answers for yourself. Letting go requires total freedom of self. The mind is quiet and free from distractions. You are here and now in the present. There is no you, just now. When you have reached this point you will begin to experience a peace and solitude that is most comforting. Allow yourself to remain in this state and begin to explore what you are looking for. The search is not taken with mind or body, it is taken with you, the eternal spirit and nothing else is part of that. Bring yourself into this light and experience what I am talking about. You are like water. When water stops flowing, it becomes stagnant and goes nowhere. For the water to flow again it needs an outlet. Once it passes through this outlet the water begins to flow again. When you become stagnant you must look for an outlet. When you find it you will begin to move in the direction of your true purpose.

What is the outlet you are looking for and how will you know when you see it?

The outlet comes when you least expect it and you are ready to see it only when you are open and receptive to its coming. The future is not ours to see but the now is where we ought to be. Being present in the now allows you to see any outlets you may pass through for greater clarity and purpose in life and for the flow of energy to be restored.

Life is Meant to Be Enjoyed

Today is a day for enjoyment. What is it that you enjoy? Bring to light those things which give you the most joy and begin to incorporate them into your life. Remember, to experience joy you must let go of worry and focus on what you want to experience. These are not difficult tasks, but when incorporated into your life they will bring you great joy and a more vibrant healthy lifestyle.

Do not be afraid to speak your mind when you feel there is something important to say. These things have been given to you for a reason, you will be able to make a great difference in the lives of other human beings.

Meditation

Not My Will Be Done but Thy Will Be Done in All Things That Are to My Highest and Greatest Good and to Those I Serve as Well.

You are to be a light for people to grow closer in. This light is the light of the world for which you seek and all others seek whether they know it or not. The light of the world is the light for which all things are possible to the highest and greatest good. There does not need to be any further conversation, for when you are in the light you are in understanding and guidance. I wish you all the peace of this day from which the light comes.

Who You Are to Become

On to you is yet another story. The story of who you are to become.

This story begins with the person you are now and evolves into the person who you are to come to know. I am the light of which you come. You have been sent here to fulfill a purpose to understand this light and from where it comes.

In your journey there will be many roads to travel but you will always travel down the road with the strongest lighted path. In this way you will begin to see your purpose more clearly and fulfill your intention. The journey is not far to travel if you stay in the light and allow yourself to be present for what is to come. Amen, I say to you, be at peace in all things and when you feel the peace is leaving you, stop and realign yourself back into it. In the absence of peace, no work or experience is worth the effort. Go and have a great day and enjoy what you have come here to do.

I am here for you, do not despair. All things come in time and when you are waiting at times it seems as if what you are seeking is not on its way. But have faith, for when you set your intention all things are given to those who have asked. Do not be concerned with whether there is a right way or wrong way of asking for what you want. Just be calm and at peace and allow it to come and it will.

To love and to have love in your heart is to be in the light. See all things with love. Place yourself inside of love, no judgment, just radiate love and you will see the light from within shining brightly. I am love, you are love and the whole world needs to achieve a greater understanding of what love and life is really all about.

In your heart know that you are love and know that you are loved. It is all a matter of perception, but no greater perception exists than the perception of true love for one's self and all others, regardless of who you perceive them to be. All is the same, all is love, not just one but also all. When you can see this you will truly be living in the light of love and understanding and your world will be filled with love and joy, free from all sickness, disease and sadness.

I am the light and through the light you will go. Do not fear the unknown and believe in your intention. When your intention is achieved, you will see the outcome. It is always based on what you had intended to manifest.

Today, I would like to tell you about the subject of peace. Why does peace leave us? Peace leaves us when we choose to accept something other than peace. How do we know when we are not at peace? We are not living in the light and we are not joyful. If you are in the light there is peace, and when there is peace there is joy, for there is nothing needed or to be concerned with. All is taken care of. Peace is like the wind, when it blows strong it is fully present. When it blows lightly it is beginning to fade away. When you notice your peace leaving you, you do not need to be concerned about how you will get it back or why you lost it. Just allow yourself to let go and be free of all attachment.

What are you holding on to that is causing your peace to fade away?

You do not need to remember, just focus on letting go of all the things you are attached to. Begin this process by letting go of attachment one step at a time. You will begin to feel lighter and more at peace. Practice this exercise until you are fully at peace with yourself and all things around you.

Quest for Finding Your Purpose

In your quest for finding your purpose, you do not have to travel very far, it is within you. You seek to accomplish many things, but are these all the things you wish to accomplish? My dear loved one, it is not what you accomplish or who you know that will fulfill your purpose. It is inside of you and it is what you learn from it that helps you to grow your soul to the next level of understanding.

If I do not wish to be in a kingdom, it is because I am not meant to be in that kingdom. My purpose lies somewhere else I am to go to fulfill my purpose. This does not mean I have to travel to find my purpose. It just means that the kingdom I am in is not where I am meant to be.

The kingdom is where you reside and place all your energy and focus to maintain its existence. To find your true purpose is to find the true kingdom where you truly belong. How do I find this kingdom? I find it by first taking a look at who I truly am. When I know who I truly am I can begin to see what purpose I came here to fulfill. There is no need for doubt or dismay for the answer is clearly seen.

Meditation

I Am Looking from Within and I Am Living On Purpose.
My Doubts, Worries and Fears Are All Gone.
I Can See My Purpose for Which I Came to Fulfill.
It Is Who I Am and What I Do That Defines Why I Am Here.
It Brings to Life What Is Necessary for Me to Grow, To Elevate Myself to The Next Level of Understanding.
I Am Truly Living, When I Am Living On Purpose.

Inside of you there are no secrets, no lies, only truth. It is from this truth that you seek understanding to further your progress along the journey of life. If we are to elevate our souls to the highest level, we are to access this very part of us to our highest and greatest good.

Seeing yourself for who you truly are is the most magnificent realization. A frog lives in the water and on land. It makes a transition from a tadpole into a frog, but this is external. What you will become is purely internal and it can't be seen through the physical representation of the body except for who you are being and how that affects your beingness.

The body is merely a shell for you to exist. It is the spirit that must manifest itself through the body to become its true form, I am. You are the very essence of what is, what was and whatever shall be. You are divine and as a divine being, you are the light of truth and of what is to become the light of the world.

Meditation

I Am Here for You Know. I Am Your Guidance.
I Am That Which Is from Within, I Am Spirit, I Am Your Guide.
If You Need Me All You Have to Do Is, Ask.
When I Am Told of Your Request, You Will Receive Guidance On That Which You Have Asked to Your Highest and Greatest Good.

What is for You or Not

If you do not receive what you have asked for, it is because the time has not come for you to receive it or it is not to your highest and greatest good. Everything is aligned so that it is in your best nature to come to know what is for you or not. It applies to things you think you should have, but only those things that are to serve you on your journey to fulfilling your path. That is your purpose in life. What you have come to learn in this lifetime.

There is no lifetime that you have come without a purpose, for this is the reason you are here. No other reason but to experience the life and purpose you designed before you came. Spirit is here to make sure that you stay on track and follow through with what you said you would do. Each and every experience is a part of the journey of fulfilling your life's purpose, that is you and who you are to become in the process. Peace is within you and all around you. But peace cannot find its way around anger. For when there is anger there is no peace. Let your mind be quiet and be at peace. If you find that this is not within you, you will know there is some anger holding you back from being at peace.

The only way you will come to know peace is to let go of all anger that you are holding onto. There can be no reason for you not to let it go. If you reason with it, you will not be able to let it go. Peace is given only when you choose to let go. Let your heart and mind and body be at peace and you will know the light of the world and experience the great joy it brings.

I know you are dissatisfied with the way things are looking now but you must be patient and allow things to unfold. In time you will come to know all things that are necessary to know. For the moment, now, you must be at peace. All things come to those who are at peace, patiently waiting for their arrival.

There is no need for worry for what is to come will seal your destiny. Be patient and wait and allow all that is to come to come and you will see the love and light that surrounds you. Do not search any further for all things are not as they appear. Do not allow your mind to interfere with who you are and who you are becoming. Enter the love and light of all that is, ever was and ever shall be. Enter the now.

On this day you shall be ever so present to the now. That is this very moment, not before or after, but the moment you are living in. Bring this present moment into existence and you will see the love and light of peace, love and understanding.

In this world you will see many changes in people but sometimes you will wonder why it is so. Do not be dismayed with the results. All people are at different stages of development in different areas of their life. One must not ever judge another's process of development, for it is their choices that direct the course of their path, and you do not have the right to interfere or judge another person for their choices.

Health

Today we shall speak about health. What is health and why is it important? Health is the state of the body. It exists in many forms. The more vibrant the body's health, the greater the capacity for communication to exist between body and spirit. When the body's health is poor it distracts the mind into believing there is no communication between body and spirit. Only the mind is in control under this false belief of poor health of body and mind.

If we are to be more vibrant in body, mind, and spirit we are to provide the body with those things that serve the body to its highest and greatest good. Natural and whole foods provide the body with what it needs to be vibrant and healthy. The foods or drinks that are not natural in substance do not provide the body with the elements of a vibrant life. When food is changed from its original state so is the body when it is digested.

Because of the change in food, there is a change in the body. This change is not for the greatest good of the body because it is unnatural. When unnatural states enter into the body, unnatural events occur. If we are to establish vibrant health we need to reestablish what we eat and drink in order to bring to the body what is natural, healthy and vibrant for the totality of vibrant health and vitality. These are the words of which we need to live by. Vibrant health and vitality exist when the body consumes vibrant, healthy whole foods and drinks. If we are to live by these guidelines, there is no need for further discussion about this topic. Live a healthy vibrant life with healthy vibrant foods.

Trust and Presence

Where can you find someone when they are missing?

You do not know what to think because you do not know where they are. You can only hope that wherever they are, that they are OK. But your mind wants to deceive you with all kinds of false beliefs. Rather than perceiving them being OK, your mind tries to make it appear that there is something wrong.

If a child is missing because someone with bad intentions has taken them, this is not what I am speaking of. I am speaking of when something is missing or someone is lost due to miscommunication, your mind begins to wonder things that are not to your highest and greatest good.

If we just believe in who we are, we have nothing to fear. All is not lost or missing, it is only absent from your presence and when it is time it may soon return. The question is why do we doubt ourselves and allow the mind to create all of these false beliefs that cause us to see the worst scenarios?

It is because we do not trust ourselves fully and we doubt what we know to be true. We rationalize, we justify to give ourselves permission to worry, because if we didn't worry there would be something wrong with us or it would show that we didn't care.

The true meaning of worry is not caring. When we doubt we begin to lose our power of who we truly are. We become weak and disconnected from all that is and ever was, the light of the world. If you can believe for one moment and not doubt and let your heart guide you, not your mind, you will begin to feel more secure. You will know that you are surrounded by the love and light of all that is, was and ever shall be. Do this now and believe in who you truly are.

Patience is a matter of being at peace with yourself. You know what is coming will come and you no longer dwell upon it. This is a matter of being present and living in the now. You are no longer attached to the past or the future. You are here right now in the moment. There is nothing to do but be present here and now.

Your life does not need to go anywhere or do anything. Just be here and now in the present. The present is all that matters and once you have entered into it, all is complete. You are truly at peace and connected to all that is, was and ever shall be. You are in the here and now, the present moment. This present moment is the gateway for peace, for living life fully with joy and great satisfaction. All is well and all is complete. There is no need for searching or understanding, just being.

How does anyone get anything accomplished by being in the present moment?

All is accomplished in the present moment that needs to be accomplished. Your life continues and you are more accessible to things that are required of you to complete. You complete them easily and freely because you are no longer attached to things that were holding you back from their full completion. You are now living the life you love and living it powerfully.

I am grateful for your presence in my life, but when I am not feeling this gratitude there appears to be something wrong. I perceive that something is missing. I am not fully at peace and somewhat disturbed. My life appears to have no direction because I am stuck in my mind.

Meditation

When I Am Trapped Inside of My Own Thoughts, I Am a Prisoner of Them and The Only Way for Me to Escape Them Is to Let Them Go and Focus On Gratitude.

My Heart Will Guide Me in What Needs to Be Done and My Mind Is Quiet as to Not to Interfere with Who I Truly Am.

I Am in The Light When I Have Let Go, And Begin to Follow My Heart.

Those Things of the Past Are No Longer a Part of My Present Reality.

I Am at Peace.

I Am at Oneness with Myself and Reality.

Therefore, There Is No Worry; I Live in The Present Moment.

I Am Grateful for Each Breath I Take.

I Allow My Life to Unfold, As It Should in The Light of Love and Peace.

Ask and It Will Be Given If You Believe

I am here today to see if there is anything you may need. All that is asked for is given if believed. What is it you would like to have in your life? I do not speak lightly when I say ask and you shall receive. What do you desire in this lifetime that you do not already have? For example, I want a car, you have a car. I want a boat, you had a boat and you sold it. I want to fly, you have been on planes before and have flown through the skies. Well, I want to be rich. You are rich in all things and those things that you lack are only because you believe you cannot have them.

You see everything has already been given to you. All you have to do is allow it to be present in your life and if it is not here right now it will come. You are not meant to live life without the fulfillment of what you desire. Your life is meant to be lived in accordance with what you have chosen. When you discover that when you choose something in life, all things are possible for those who believe in it.

If it is not in direct alignment with your life and you ask for something not for yourself but for another person, the person must truly accept what you have asked for with no doubt or disbelief. These are the words by which you must live by if you wish to be abundant in this lifetime.

Meditation

I Am Abundant to This Lifetime and Always.

My Abundance Is Mine to Receive and to Give to Another.

When I Choose to Believe, My Abundance Is Mine to Receive, No One Can Take It Away.

It Is an Endless Reservoir, In Accordance to My Belief.

I Am Grateful for All Things to My Highest and Greatest Good for in Which I Receive in This Lifetime or Any Other.

The Outcome

If you wish to learn something, you must first decide on what you intend to achieve by doing it. First, you must know what is the final outcome. Only when the outcome is known do you have a purpose for achieving the results you desire. If you do not know how to do something, examine what is involved in it before starting. Know what each step is and how long it will take you to complete the task. Estimation is fine for those of you who wish perfection.

When you have a clear understanding of what is involved in doing something and how long it will take, you decide to do it or not. Do not be caught up with asking yourself whether or not you should do it. Go through the steps and decide, yes or no, based on what you have found out.

No details are necessary, no agenda, just begin when you are ready. In beginning a task, you must know approximately how many steps are involved. Once you do this all you need to do is focus on one step at a time. As you complete each step you will see the progress made and be able to know that it will be completed.

The important thing to remember here is to stay focused on the step you are on and know the outcome. The outcome is your reason for doing what you are doing. If you do not know the outcome, there can be no real reason for doing something and this will sometimes cause you to not complete what you have started.

Staying focused on what you have started is a matter of staying focused on the outcome. When you know something is coming you are always more motivated to do what needs to be done, because you know it will arrive. In completing the task, you have completed the outcome. No other task is needed to move forward except for another outcome. With each outcome you achieve you move closer to your final outcome, which is your purpose in this lifetime.

I do not know what it is you want to achieve. But the greatest achievement is being present in the here and now. For when you are being present in the moment, life is joyful and all can be achieved. Do not worry for what is to come. Just focus on the present moment and you will know what best to do.

It is your worry that is stopping you from any achievement. Therefore, be present in the moment, connect to nature, silence the mind and notice what is present. You will experience joy and this joy is the present moment.

There is no darkness in light. Light can only exist in the presence of peace and love. This love is for all things whether good or bad, there is no judgment in love. There is just love. It comes from the heart and it is guided through the heart, not the mind. There is no thinking here. Love is the expression of who we truly are and it is communicated through the heart, not the mind. When we love, we are inviting into our life the light of all that is, ever was and ever shall be. This eternal peace comes from the eternal source of love and light, this is the true understanding of what is and cannot be expressed in any other way than love.

Meditation on Love

Love Is Kind and Patient. It Does Not Speak with Anger.
Love Seeks to Embrace Not Detach.
It Is the Light of All Good and The Eternal Peace of Joy and Happiness.
Love Is Present When One Is Willing to Let Go and Allow Love to Flow from The Heart Freely, With No Thought or Judgment of Any Kind.

Today you are to take notice of what is and what is not. By this we mean what is real and what is not real. Take notice of the flower and see if it appears real to you. Take notice of a book on your desk or shelf and ask, what is the message here and am I receiving the truth or not? What is real is what you can see light in. There is no light in what is not real. By light, I am speaking of all that is, ever was and ever shall be. I am speaking of the truth of all that is. What is real is real because it has light around it. No matter how much light it has, it is real.

Not all things have the same light. Some have more, some have less. It is all according to how much light is allowed in. When there is light there is truth and when there is truth there is room for more light — the light of the eternal source of all that is. You see you must not doubt that the light of one is not the same as another. We are all traveling the same path. Although some may take longer than others to get there. The eternal source of light is always willing to wait and allow as much time as needed to arrive at the proper destination.

I am here today to discuss peace. Peace in the heart, peace of the mind and peace of the body. Peace does not come from within. It comes from a place where one can reside without any conflict of mind, body and heart. All is well. All is at peace because the mind is quiet and free from distraction.

The body is at rest and remains still and calm and the heart is filled only with love for all things whether good or bad, there is no judgment here. All things remain at peace because all things are working together for the same purpose and that purpose is to enter into the divine light of personal consciousness.

By personal, we mean without any distraction from the external or internal world. The state of being that occurs when a mother holds her child for the first time, all that is experienced is love and the peace that surrounds it.

Love Mediation II

Love Is Kind.
Love Is Patient.
Love Does Not Seek Reward.
It Is Just It Is Fair.
Love Seeks to Connect All Things Together as One.
Love Is the Only Path That Will Light Your Way to Goodness and Great Joy.
There Is No Fear.
There Is No Doubt.
There Is Just Love.

In Appearance

Today is a day for you to understand the meaning of sorrow. We are speaking of sorrow in terms of loss of a loved one. When we are in love we are connected as one. When a partner loses a loved one there is an absence of that oneness in mind, not body. The one who experiences the sorrow of loss believes they have lost that oneness that they had with their loved one.

It is not so, the connection remains and so does the oneness. But it is the mind that perceives that it no longer remains. We do this because we are attached to the body and we don't realize that we are spirit.

Spirit never dies. Therefore, there is no sorrow or separation. The oneness remains and the connection with spirit remains. You cannot be separated from spirit unless you ask for it to be so. But no spirit is disconnected from a loved one because it has left the body. The spirit remains present with its loved one and continues to be connected until such time where both spirits are united out of body and into spirit.

These are the words of the most high. Live life with your loved one in body and spirit, and when body is no longer connected know that spirit remains and sorrow is only for the loss of the body but not of the spirit.

Love Meditation III.

Love Is Kind.
Love Is Patient.
Love Is Without Anger.
For in Love, You Can Do Many Things.
Out of Love, You Are in A Series of Struggles with Yourself and Others.
Do Not Be Persuaded to Follow the Second Path.
For to Be Out of Love Is to Be Lost and Disconnected from All That Is Good Just and True.

Focus Your Attention on Your Heart

Focus your attention on your heart and allow love to come forth. Onto you will be love and light of the most high. From love and light there is no darkness and all things are as they should be. Bring forth this love in all things and you will see your life as it should be. To your highest and greatest good.

If your life is not the way you want it, it is because you have created it to be that way. Everything you say do and achieve is a direct result of what goes in your head and is what you have created. If you are a creator, everything you say with power and belief is a part of your creation. I am that which you are. Everything comes from the source of light and love. In you I am. If we are to create what we would like to experience, we are to focus our minds on believing that it is already ours to come. There is no beginning or ending. All there that exists is right now. In the now comes your source of all creation. I am here right now, I am. Let not your heart be worried, trust in the I am, and all that you ask will be given to you to your highest and greatest good.

If you would like to experience moving forward in life you must first move in love and peace. Through love and peace all things are possible. You do not have to worry how and why things are to be done. Are you not satisfied with who you are? Why do you try so hard to become someone you are not? In you I am and that is all that matters. From the I am, you are a creator. One who creates what who you believe is possible.

If you wish to be loved, be love. Do not let your mind guide you. Be guided by your heart. If we are to experience love in our lives, we must be open to it. Let your love unfold within you and you will see its power. Love does not misguide you. It will heal you and direct you to your highest and greatest good. In this we speak the words of the most high. Love they neighbor as thy self. Love as you wish to be loved. Be love, to your highest and greatest good. Love is the cause of all things good, be love, give love, receive love and the peace of God will follow you everywhere you go.

Live your life in love with love. Let love surround you wherever you go. You can choose to see what is wrong but that is not love and it will not bring the peace or joy that you seek.

When love is present there is no judgment. Love provides you with peace and joy. In a state of love, you feel content and happy. You do not require reasons why something is not so. Bring your attention fully on the state of love. Bring love and surround yourself and others with love, to your highest and greatest good of all people.

Live Life in Love

If your life is not the way you wish it to be, recreate it in the way you would like to experience it. In love one can experience the ultimate joy of life. In love all things are possible. We are at peace and we are able to manifest our desires freely.

Living a life in love is living a life you love. There is no tomorrow and there is no today. All that exists is the here and now. The present moment is where all peace, love and joy can be found. Are you not aware of the present moment and how powerful it really is?

Take your life to the present moment and you will find peace, love and joy. It is within the present moment that we truly live our lives with personal freedom. We are able to make clear decisions without constraints. All I ask is that you listen and be still in the present moment and allow the peace, love and joy to flow. When you are in the present moment you will understand its power. If you do not practice you will not remain in this state of mind. Therefore, daily practice is important to manifest your desires and maintain the present flow of life's existence.

Let light flow through you as light comes from the sun. When there is light there is no darkness. If we are to live in light, we are to live with love in our hearts. Love fills the heart with light and through this light love flows. There is no greater light than love.

If love does not exist light does not come through. In order for love to exist, peace must be present. As peace comes so does love. In love, we are all one connected to one love and one light.

It is so easy to let go of what really matters. We become distracted from that which we truly love. We have life experiences and yet we truly do not learn what is most important. We become distracted with life's experiences. How do we become so lost in a world we have come to know and experience? If we just let go and live life from love in all our circumstances, how joyful we would become now? In our heart we can feel it.

Love does exist. Its presence makes us who we truly are. Allow love to flow from within you. Bring forth all of its beauty and joy, for you are one and the same as I am.

Love rejoices within you. It comes forth as a shining light that surrounds you. It brings forth a great sense of peace and joy as you begin to let go of all that is not love. It flows like a mighty river and it comes within you like a majestic waterfall. You are overflowing with love and peace, joy and fulfillment. I am that which you are. The love light of the world. To your highest and greatest good in peace, love, and joy.

Do not worry what it is you are supposed to do or what you think you should do. Focus your attention on love. This is when your heart will rejoice in what you are doing and being. Love brings all things to all kinds of people. Love heals and love brings tremendous joy. For when there is love you are whole and complete. There is no separation of self from that which is all love. The divine is with you and you are with the divine.

All love is connected to one love that is the one and only true love. This love is all-encompassing and it does not deny anyone's calling if it truly comes from their heart. In love you are one with the divine. When you are one with the divine you are whole and complete. Inside of love there is the heart of forgiveness and understanding. There exists a level of compassion like no other. This compassion is all healing and all giving and it is through this love that one becomes whole and complete. You begin to discover who you truly are, one with the divine. As I have said, you do not need to look for what to do or think of what you should do. Just focus your attention on love and all that you desire will come through without effort or delay. In love with the divine is like being in love with yourself and sharing that love with all others to the highest and greatest good of all kind.

Let your heart be still. Do not allow anything to steer you away from the light. Be at peace and choose peace in all things. When you are in the light, love remains. If you are not living a life you love you are not living life as you should. All life is meant to be enjoyed and to be a joyful experience. It is this life that you expand your soul's capacity to grow.

All growth is in our learning experiences. As we begin to have experiences we begin to learn the lessons for our soul's growth. As we begin to expand more and more our soul begins to understand more of what it means to experience these lessons. These lessons are learned in order for us to grow. The experiences are not given to us if we do not wish to participate.

All experiences exist for a purpose in which we are to move forward in life. I am is that which you seek, if you seek the I am you are seeking that which is in the light. Let love be your guide and do not trust in those things that appear to be real — like false hope and fear. Fear is the underlying cause of doubt. Do not trust in fear and you will have no doubt. Your purpose will be clear and you will seek only the truth, which is your one and only true guide.

After you understand what it means to be fearless, you can begin to live a life you love and live it powerfully. For now, it is up to you to seek that which is only in the light. The one and only true source of guidance for life.

State your Intention

If you are to live a life you love and live it powerfully it is up to you to choose peace in every circumstance and experience. By choosing peace you are stating your intention. In this you will remain in the light in every manner of circumstance. If we are to choose peace and remain in the light, there is no need to search for answers. Our guidance will always show us the way. In peace we remain open to understanding our true path and direction. All is well and all is right in the light from which we come. Our path is designated in certain respects. Through guidance, love and light, we begin to see the clearest and most direct path to get to our final destination.

The End in Mind

If there is something you wish to do, stop thinking about it and do it. One step at a time you will get there as long as you can see the end in mind and not be stuck in your own thinking. When you are stuck in your own thinking — meaning you are not taking actions — you will remain in stagnation. There is no movement forward because you have not initiated the first step.

Do not worry about whether something can or cannot be done. You will find a way as long as you have set your intentions and believe in the outcome as if it already is so. You may not be able to predict when you will achieve your results but belief does ensure they are coming.

There is no greater source of power than when you already believe your outcome is on its way. The power you receive from believing in your intentions will make you unstoppable and you will no longer doubt your abilities. All is well and all is coming.

What is it that you would like to experience most in your life?

Set your intentions and believe that it is already on its way. You will see great things occurring that you never knew existed. The love and light of all things will shine upon you to your highest and greatest good.

The Presence of Peace

In life there is but one thing that is most important and that is love. There is no greater gift than the gift of love. Giving and receiving love is life's greatest reward. Move forward in life in the spirit of peace, love and joy and you will see great things happen to your highest and greatest good.

To live a life we love, we must live it peacefully and without judgment. All judgement comes from seeing things as if they are not already perfect, as if there is something wrong that we're trying to fix. To better understand ourselves we need to understand judgment can interfere with our ability to see things clearly.

What causes us not to be joyful and happy?

Joy is the presence of peace and calm. It does not desire anything but to be still. To manifest joy in your life you must give up judgment in all forms. Judgment takes you away from your freedom to experience joy. Joy is not just having fun or being playful. It is a combination of things that lead to the full experience of what it means to be joyful. I have joy when I am at peace with all things and I am free of all judgment. My desire to be free of judgment must be intentional. If I am attached to a problem or circumstance, I am not free. Attachment is not letting go of something. It is a form of judgment. We usually remain attached to something because we feel entitled to be right about what we are perceiving to be true. We justify our beliefs by claiming what we believe is the truth. But it is a false perception. As a result, we remain a victim to our own judgments. We suffer and feel pain that we are creating by wanting to be right.

When we become a victim, we lose our power, and there is no joy or freedom. Our experience is one of pain, regret or guilt. We are stuck in a vacuum of our own making because we refuse to let go of any judgments we are attached to. It does not matter whether the experience we had was right or wrong. If we remain attached to an experience of the past that no longer exists, we also remain stuck in pain, sorrow or regret.

How can we experience the true joy of living a life we love?

If we are not willing to let go of the past, the past will rule us and steal all of our joy and love. The ironic part of this is that we are in control if we just let go and choose not to remain attached to false perceptions. You must understand that life is based on free will and it is through our choosing that we remain in the results we experience. We must let go of judgments and desires to be right about something we truly cannot own. We cannot experience true joy until we are willing to let go of the past and live in a present that has no judgment toward things we experience. The moment we let go we begin to live a life to our highest and greatest good.

Meditation

I am the source of all light.
Through me light passes through.
Let there be peace and calm in my heart, body and mind.
Allow me to be judgment free so that I now experience a greater sense of the joy that flows through me now.
I let go of the past and all judgments that held me prisoner to experiencing the full love and light I experience now.
I am judgment free.
I am experiencing the peace, love and joy of letting go of all attachment that are known and unknown to me in my life now.
I am now fully in communion with the divine love and light of the most high and powerful to my highest and greatest good.

The Light of Compassion

Inside of love lies a light of compassion and understanding that brings goodness to the heart. This feeling is vitalizing the spirit to come out to its highest and greatest good. One does not need to understand this process but only know that it exists and allow it to unfold. The feeling of love and light in one's heart is overwhelming and causes one to experience great joy. You do not need to force it to come out. All you need is to be open and receptive to its presence and it will come forth in its own way. One does not need to do anything but sit still and be and quiet the mind. All is given to those who are open to receive. Bring forth this love and light in your heart now and see the great joy it brings to your highest and greatest good.

What's Stopping Me from Doing What I Love?

There is nothing stopping you from doing what you love but your own perceptions. You are perceiving the world in a certain way and as a result you are creating your own experience. Let go of things you don't want and you will begin to perceive your world in a whole different way. Your world will become a world you love to live in and it will provide you great love, peace and joy.

Now let us begin to see what is missing so you can begin creating a life you love and live it powerfully. As you begin to live a life you love you begin to see what is most important. In life there is only one way to live and that is through being peaceful and calm. This does not mean you can't do exciting things and achieve magnificent results beyond your wildest imagination. Being calm and peaceful is a state of mind that allows you to bring a result more easily, because there is nothing in your way to block you. Inside a state of peace and calm lies the freedom to create whatever you would like to experience. When you come to know that, you can create anything you believe in. Life becomes a most joyful experience. It is through our perceived limitations that we create a life of struggle and despair. We believe we are not in control and therefore we are helpless and cannot see the light. If we are not in the light, we are in darkness and through darkness we cannot live a life we love. Life is not meant to be hard, but it is through our own minds and thoughts that we make it so. Our reality is an illusion that we believe as true.

If we need to free our minds from all the illusions and perceptions that are creating our reality, how do we do this?

One step at a time and with great intention. It is our intentions that guide our reality and when we are clear on what our intentions are, we can move forward with creating a life we love and living it powerfully. Living a life you love is a world in which you live. False illusions and perceptions are not part of a world in which you live a life you love and live it powerfully. Let's take the first step toward living a life you love and living it powerfully to your highest and greatest good.

Breaking Free of the Human Condition

How do we live our lives each day?

We live our lives each day by the way we have become conditioned. We have lost our ability to see and hear the true essence and beauty of love and joy. Our attachments to human conditions hold us back from seeing who we truly are, the love and light of the world. Yet as we have come to know what is lost can be found. Only through direct guidance can we truly see the light. We have become so attached to our human conditions that we have forgotten how to be in alignment with our true nature. It is the essence of who we are that matters.

Our human conditions are only experiences that we have come to know and believe as the real truth. But when we die we come to understand what is the most important aspect of our lives. We come to know we are connected to one source, the love and light of all worlds. It is through this source that the true essence of who we are manifests us as spiritual beings. As spiritual beings we are one and the same source of light and love. As humans we have lost or forgotten how to remain connected to our true essence. We do not take the time or we have forgotten how to reconnect to this one source of love and light. We remain stuck in our human condition of a false reality.

Getting unstuck is not impossible. All that is required is an intention to go to a place of solitude and be still and allow your true essence to come out.

What prevents us from being still and allowing our true essence to come out?

The human condition and the attachment to beliefs prevents one from experiencing his or her true essence. You are not alone, but it is your free will that chooses to remain stuck in the human condition or to let go and allow the manifestation of your true self to come forth.

We are speaking of the love and light of the most high to be the main source of inspiration in your life. You do not live your life from a human condition but from the source of all love and light. In this we give you your true essence of a spiritual being, love and light to you highest and greatest good.

Love's Presence in Your Heart

As you being each day, begin with love in your heart. If you do not feel love's presence in your heart sit quietly and allow love's presence to unfold from within you. The very intention of having love in your heart is all that is required. You do not need to read or look for inspiration. Just be still, and allow love's presence to unfold. Love's presence does not need to be called upon for any reason. It is always available to anyone who asks. The purpose of love in your heart is to manifest your true desires to live a life you love in peace and calm.

It does not matter who you are or what you have done. Love is all giving and unconditional. Open your heart to love's presence and you will truly find it. Now let us begin with who you are.

You are not separate from love. Everything that you are is a part of love. Love does not exist for some it is for all. For love is a part of all things. When you ask "How can love be of all things?" you are not seeing love's true essence. When we cannot see love's presence it is because we are blinded by the human condition.

We see only false illusions of the behaviors we are portraying from our own experiences. If we are to truly experience love and see it all around us we must see with eyes of love. Seeing with eyes of love does not pass judgment upon another. Seeing with eyes of love is unconditional.

Why do we see others as not good enough?

Because we believe we are not good enough. So we believe in the illusion we are not whole and complete and that love is something outside of ourselves. Seeing with eyes of love is unconditional love.

It is our human condition that covers up love's true essence. When we stop believing in the illusion that we are not already whole and complete, we can assume our role as truly loving spiritual beings.

Being loving is being at peace with one's self. If I am at peace with myself I am already whole and complete. I do not need to search for what is missing to make me complete. As a result, when I am already whole and complete I begin to see others as whole and complete.

I can begin to experience what unconditional love truly means. I love others as myself without judgment, unconditionally. We say live a life you love and live it powerfully through loving yourself and others unconditionally to your highest and greatest good.

If love does not exist in your life you must find it. Love is everywhere. It is in the sky, the moon, the stars and the sun, it is all around us. In order to feel love's presence, you must empty yourself of all distraction and place yourself in the presence of love. There is nothing to do but be in a state of presence.

When you find love you will know it. It is a warm peaceful feeling that is so delightful you never want to let go. Its presence fills you with a sense of peace and quiet like no other. Love is the source of all things and when you are in love's presence you are in the flow.

Do not wait for love's presence to come. Allow yourself to be in love's presence all of the time. Live your life from love and you will see a world from a whole new perspective, to your highest and greatest good.

If you are to love, your first love should begin with yourself. Loving yourself is key to true love because you must first love yourself before you can love anyone else. Love must be present in yourself before you can give it to someone else. If we ignore this simple rule we will not fully experience love's presence.

What more can you give yourself than loving yourself?

It is the greatest service one can offer. In love, all things are possible. So begin loving yourself today and you will receive love's greatest reward.

Is Love All That Really Matters?

Yes. When there is love there is joy and peace. What matters more than to have joy and peace is one's life? To seek a life we love, we must seek it through love. We do this by being loving and compassionate toward all things.

We are allowing ourselves to be in love with life when we are loving and at peace. Joy comes to us easily and freely. Life begins to flow in a whole new way, one that is natural and to our highest and greatest good. Be in love with love and let this be your guiding principle for living a life you love.

Please bring to light all that you love. When you are in love with love there can be no greater feeling. Sit still for a moment and bring all that you love into the present moment. Notice how you feel when you are in love. Love does not care about the past or the future. Love's only concern is the present moment of now.

If you are in love with love you are truly in the present moment. Live life to your highest greatest good in love.

If all is OK, all is well. But why do we assume something must be wrong? If we live a life we love, we must be at peace and know all is well and there is nothing wrong. What causes doubt and disbelief is our ability to create illusions that are not real. Doubt and disbelief are symptoms of an illusion. We believe in a story we created and believe it as our reality. In the context of peace and love you do not choose to create such stories because you choose peace and love instead.

To realize our true selves, we must choose peace and love in all circumstances and allow compassion to fill our lives. The moment we begin to hold judgment toward something, we are no longer experiencing peace, love and joy in our lives.

I do not say to ignore what is happening, but to simply observe it though the eye of peace, love and compassion. When we do this we are truly living a life we love. Joy, peace and love is all around us. To your highest and greatest good.

Let your heart not worry about anything. Be still and at peace. Through presence you will know actions to take and life will be joyful. If you wonder why you are not where you are supposed to be it is because you have lost contact with the present moment. In this moment is all that matters and if you are not here right now you are lost. Inspiration takes place in the present moment when you are ready to receive it. Inspiration cannot exist elsewhere. If you desire to understand something, be in the present moment and allow inspiration to come through when it is ready. You cannot force results to come. You must allow inspiration to come. Just set your intention and be in the present moment. All that matters is now, nothing further than this is required.

In love all things are possible. Do all things in love and you will see love's power. To live a life you love you must live from love in all things. Love is not difficult but it does require presence in what you are doing and being. In whatever you are doing, love most reside. Living a life you love without love's presence is not living a life. Stop becoming so distracted with so many different things. Love does not require you to do a lot. All love asks is that you be present in the here and now and look no further than that.

Love's very nature is to be still. It does not require more. So let love be your guide. Allow love to come from the heart and you will surely live a life you love and live it powerfully to your highest and greatest good.

Live Life in Love

To live life in love you must choose peace always. You choose peace by being judgment free. Have no judgment toward anyone or anything. If you choose to serve, have no expectation, give from the heart and allow love to flow through. In this way you will truly know you are living life in love to your highest and greatest good.

Love is the only thing that really matters. You must be at peace for love's presence to reside within you. Let go of all forms of judgment. In this you will know truth and what it means to live a life in love.

Know that there is love in all things. Be open to see love. When you see love you are more able to receive it openly and freely. Inside of your life there is so much to learn. One step at a time will get you there. There is no need to worry or to rush. All is given to you in due time.

There is no need for hurry or panic. Take one step at a time until you have achieved your desired results. Focus on one, not many activities at a time. When you have completed one project you may go onto the next.

If you have too many projects at the same time you will not achieve anything because your time will be dispersed, causing you to lose focus and momentum. Just as no two things can occupy the same space at the same time, it is wise to do the same in your activities and projects.

Projects and activities are just a means for occupying time and space. They do not create love and joy unless one lives their life through love. This is why we speak of love as your primary focus. For all things come from love and through love all things are possible. We need to look at this in a holistic way. Love is the central theme and all else will follow if you remain in love.

Love heals all things. Through love you will heal. There is no pain in love. There is no sorrow, for when love is present it brings goodness and peace.

Only through peace and love can someone truly heal. Bring the love and light around you and you will begin to feel the peace and healing take place. Do not hold on to sorrow or pain. Let it go and surrender to the peace and love of the most high and divine. Do not live in your pain or sorrow.

Live in love and peace will follow you wherever you go. It is not yesterday that matters, only the now. Through this very moment you can find peace and love in your heart if you surrender and let go and allow peace and love to flow freely in your heart. I deliver this to you, now live in the light of peace and love in all things to your highest and greatest good always.

If you are in denial of your true self, it is to your highest and greatest good to come to know who you truly are. Once this is realized you will come to know peace and love in all areas of your life. There is no darkness, only peace and love. For when you enter into the light only light prevails. Darkness does not come where there is light. There are only lessons to be learned. When we learn these lessons we can chose to learn them in peace, love and light, or in darkness that usually prevents the true understanding of what is to be learned.

If we are in darkness the only course of action is to let go and surrender to the peace, love and light of the most high. There is no way of doing this if one is not willing to let go of their pain and sorrow. I pray that you live your life though peace, love and light. When there is sorrow or pain, surrender to peace, love and light and let God's will be done.

As we have said before, love is all that really matters. If you can live your life in love you can live a life of peace, love and joy. There is no need for worry, doubt or fear. For when there is love in your heart you are whole and complete. Your actions and thoughts are always guided to your highest and greatest good.

Why do you need to worry about things other than love?

These things will not bring you joy. Love is all that matters. If you are a carpenter and you love making things out of wood this is what you do, and through this work you make your living and live a life you love. It is not meant to be complicated. It is only though fear and doubt that we become confused, love lights the way to clarity and purpose.

Your purpose should be what you love and what you love should be your guide for living a life you love. Through peace and love you will see all things clearly. I ask that you now seek to do the things that you love to the highest and greatest good of all including yourself.

There are so many things I love. How do I know which things to focus on without becoming overwhelmed? You must choose to focus your attention on one thing at a time and stay focused on that particular choice until you have achieved the desired outcome. This is why you should always take time to visualize your outcome so that you already know what you desire before it is manifested.

Seeing the outcome gives you a clear picture of what you truly desire and will let you know if it is something you truly want to spend your time on. Allow yourself to spend time on imagining the outcome and seeing the whole picture. Once you can see the final outcome you will more than likely know which steps to take to produce the desired results. Bringing these results into your reality is all a matter of perception and belief.

If you do not create the vision and belief for what you would like to manifest, you are always wondering whether you are on the right track. Creating a clear image in your mind of your desired results will be is the fastest way to manifest what you would like to experience in your life.

As you begin to live your life, live your life from your creative imagination to create what you would like to achieve to your highest and greatest good.

What Life Is

In life you will see many avenues and streets, they move in different directions. The direction you take is in accordance with what you are thinking at that particular time. One is drawn to different streets or avenues of life because energy and thought take them down that path.

Can we change which direction we will go?

We can only change how we think about a particular subject by focusing our mind differently. We do this by letting go and allowing the freedom within us to reside. When we are free from within we are truly free to choose which path will suit us best. The past is not the present or the future. The past is what has been and is no longer.

The only reason the past remains is because it is allowed to remain, stored in the mind. The mind has not let go of the past due to its attachment to memories, trauma or pain. The mind wants to hold onto the past because it feels that if it lets it go it will lose something of value that cannot be replaced.

Even though this is not the truth the mind believes it to be so. It stays attached to past memories, trauma and pain. The only way the mind can release the past is by allowing it to be let go.

When the mind lets go of the past it discovers a new freedom that did not exist. It has let go of attachment and is no longer controlled by the past. This allows for freedom to be in the present because nothing is in its way. We can see letting go of the past is one of the main foundations for truly establishing freedom in one's life — the freedom to be who you are in the here and now.

Please understand you are not in the present until you have fully let go of all past experiences that have caused you to lack understanding in true guidance. As you remain in the past you will always know there is something more, something that you are searching for but it cannot exist until you have left the past and have become fully present in the here and now.

You will know you are in the present when you no longer have the desire to search for something more. You are content with the here and now and nothing matters further. In regards to your worldly life, this must continue with obligations and commitments you have made. It is not advisable to let go of everything and fall into an abyss of nothingness.

As you are in this world you are still connected to its ways and as a result it is your obligation to live your life within these guidelines.

I am that from which you are, that is I am. In you I am, there is no we, only I for we are all connected. In your world you see much separation because man has chosen to be separate, but they are never really separate — in mind and body, but not in spirit.

Because of free will, you have been given the choice where you will begin and where you will go. There is no separation in who you are and in who you become. Leave behind your ways of thinking that you are separate and become one with the I am. Fear will not allow you to do this because you and so many have been misguided for so long. When you are ready to begin, start by becoming connected to that which you know to be true and leave behind the false beliefs you were told were true. You are now entering into oneness of I am, where the false beliefs no longer reside and only truth can prevail.

Why have you become who you are?

You have become who you are because of your thinking. When connected to source this thinking no longer remains, it is something of the past and begins to fade away. How you know this to be true is things were not the same in appearance as they are now. Because of your desire to become connected to source you have chosen a path to enlightenment. This path is not of the world and remains within the context of source. I am, that is who you are. If this is not clear it will soon become your guiding principle. No longer do you live in the past of who am I? You now live in the present of I am. Please understand that there is no point for you to reach and that all things come in time. If you are uncertain, be patient, for when you are peaceful there is more room for understanding and true guidance.

In Touch with Spirit

Today is a day for being in touch with spirit. By spirit, I mean your higher self which is you. You are to understand that you are not the body but you are spirit and the body's function is to serve the spirit. This is why we represent the body as a temple of God.

Whatever you may be thinking about who you really are is not relevant to this topic. The body exists for the spirit to reside. In this case it is the spirit that leaves the body when the body is at rest or when the body is no longer of service. We all have our purpose and when that purpose is fulfilled, the spirit leaves the body. But the spirit is still the spirit, it does not die it only moves on to experiences of another kind. In this we can see that the spirit is always alive living in this world and the next.

There is no need for disruption of service, because the spirit always remains present and a part of the one true source of power that exists in every individual. This source is I am, that which is you. We do not speak of mountains, which appear to be a place of rest. The mountains only store what's inside of them and do not serve any purpose but to bring the earth's surface to its highest point that is within reach of all of us.

Therefore, when we are standing on the mountain, we are standing on a place we know no longer exists. When we let go of all that is below us, we begin to rise to a higher consciousness. This higher consciousness resides within all of us and is dormant for the most part when the spirit enters the body.

It can only open itself when it comes to the realization that all is one and that the body is merely a temple in which the spirit remains in for a period of time. No longer are you to remain in the body disconnected from the spirit. You are now rising from the body to higher consciousness and higher awareness of another kind. I am for you and you and I are the same, I am.

We do not speak of division, but oneness and that divine essence that is you and everything around you. I am complete when there is no you, but only I am, the eternal, the source, the light and center of who we truly are. Bring to this moment your higher state of consciousness and reside there on top of the mountain and you will begin to see a world unlike your own — from which all love and light comes from and is always and forever present.

I am the light, I am the way, the source of all your problems lies within. Let go and you will see problems no longer remain. Let go by letting go of all concerns of the past. Be in the present not the past. You are truly blessed and much will be given to you, just be patient and allow it to happen. Your state of presence is key. Remain in this state and if you find yourself not present, bring yourself back and just let go of all that lies in your way.

In you I am, and the love and light will shine.

Stay focused on your heart and how things feel, no mind just heart. From the heart comes love and light and the understanding that will guide you on your path. There is no need for worry or doubt, just faith and belief that I am in you. In you I am and when you believe, no further actions need to be taken.

Inspiration will come from within and you will be guided in this way. No longer do you need to search to find the answers, everything needed is already from within. Do not follow the world and how it tells you what you should do or the way it is done. The only way something is done is how you choose to have it done. We have been told that if we do not do things in a certain way we cannot acquire results. This is for those who live by the world and are guided by the world not spirit. When you allow inspiration to come from within you are truly creating the life you were meant to live. Life becomes the way you create it to be, not the other way around.

You were meant to create and in creating you create your life and what it is you came here to learn. There can be no greater source of satisfaction in this world than to fulfill your purpose, what you were meant to be.

What if you knew you only had three days to live?

What would you do? Would you celebrate, would you pray, would you say goodbye to all those you love? It is not difficult to know you would do things that are most important to you.

You would not waste your time in idle chatter and you would not spend a lot of time just thinking. You would make decisions as quickly as possible so you could have an experience and move on to the next. You would not want to waste time with indecision because you'd know your time was running out.

So where do you begin?

You begin by choosing one thing at a time and moving to the next until you have finished as many as you could. Now you are down to the last hour of your life. What will you do? If you decide to go somewhere you will spend some of your time in travel and this might not be the best use of your time. Though you could spend travel time in appreciation for what you had in your life if the destination was of great importance.

Let's say you've decided not to travel and your last hour will begin in the next 30 seconds. Have you decided yet? I did. I would spend my last hour in love and appreciation of all the things I have experienced whether good or bad, knowing that all were for a lesson and for a greater understanding of who I am and what I have become. I would ask for God's blessing and grace to remember all that I needed to remember so I could show my gratitude.

Finally, when it is the last minute of my life I would breathe deeply knowing that my life is not over and that I am just about to begin a new journey into a new world of existence. Leaving my body behind I am still who I am, that is me. I continue to live, but I am on a different plane of existence. I am here and I am somewhere else. I continue to learn who I am and who I have become. I am the you that is I and the I that is me, I am the one.

Rekindle Your Spirit

Today is a day like no other. It is a day to rekindle your spirit for the greater good of those you serve in this lifetime. To rekindle is to restart, ignite like a fire in the night. The reason is simple. It is for you to see the power of the light and love that is within you.

A rekindling process begins with "I love you," and it proceeds with sparks that will ignite a passion that burns until you are no more in this body. Understand that when you ignite the fire from within it will serve you for all your days.

Do not worry how or why it will begin, just know it has already started and in time you will understand its full significance. For now, just begin your day as you normally would and begin to see the sparks of light. The process is simple and will not take long, but you must allow it to occur one step at a time. With each step you will see the fire.

Today is a great day of importance. It is a time of significant change. In you there lies a potential for greatness. This greatness is beginning to manifest itself from within. It has always been there but has been in a dormant state.

As we begin this day we begin a new transition in your life. There is no need to worry or suffer the pain of everyday frustrations, just allow them to be and see what is the lesson to be learned. This is not a joy ride. Much understanding will come in many different ways. But in all things when there is love and light there is no need for worry or pain from the agony of uncertainty.

We are pleased you have come this far and continue to move forward. We are delighted to see the progress that is being made each day as you pass through each experience. Stay in the light in all things and you will find an understanding and peace. If you are in darkness let there be light. Always bring forth the greater understanding of peace love and light. Begin each day with this in mind.

Meditation

The Love and Light of Peace Fills My Day in All That I Do and in All That I Learn.
I Am in The Light for My Highest and Greatest Good.
I Seek to Make a Difference and to Live a Life in The Light of Peace, Love and Presence.
In This, I Am Truly Who I Am.
Joy Fills My Heart for I Am No Longer Attached to The Past or The Future.
I live in the present moment.
In You, I Am and in I Am, I Am.

I Love You

There is no love in darkness. Love is only in the light. When one focuses on love one is in the light. Love is the surrendering of oneself to all things. It is not a justification for physical pleasure.

Although physical pleasure does come with love, this is not the type of love about which we are speaking. The love we are speaking about is all giving and does not bring darkness, only light. It is giving for it is true love, the kind that can only be giving while in the light. If you do not wonder what it really is, you will never know the great joy it brings. For when in love, you are in light and the love carries you through all things because you are at peace with all things.

In our life we know love from the love of God that brings his only begotten son into the world as a savior for all mankind. If mankind is to be saved, they are to love as the savior did, to give of oneself for the greater good of all humanity.

There is no expectation to receive something in return. There is only love, there is only giving freely without any expectation for a reward. This is true love, and there can be no greater love than this. Open your heart and give freely of yourself without any expectation of what you will receive.

When you do this you are truly in love with yourself and all others in this world. Go forth and love as you have never loved before. The state of not being in the light separates you from who you truly are and who you truly want to be. How do we let go of uncertainty? You begin to look at what is causing the disconnection and asking yourself why am I attached to this state of being?

You will quickly realize what is causing this separation. Once you begin to see the cause you can begin to let it go and once again make your way back into the light.

Meditation

Love Is Kind.
Love Is Giving.
Love Is Being Open to Receive but for All Things, Love Is the Light from Which You Came.
In Love There Is No Darkness Only Light.
When Love Is Present There Is Light.
When There Is Light There Is the True Presence of All That Is Ever Was and Ever Shall Be.

So how do we remain in a state of love? We remain in a state of love by giving ourselves completely. We do not look for rewards, we just give of ourselves. When we can give freely with no concern for what we will receive we are beginning to love more freely without constraints.

Love does not bring on concerns of the past, its only concern is with the present here and now. If we do not love, we do not see the light. The only way in is to let go of the past and be in the present. If we are to go into the night without love, we will remain in darkness, not truly knowing the way we are to proceed in life.

Life is simple. It does not need to be difficult. We make it difficult by being attached to the past and not being in the here and now. When you are present you are happy, you experience love for all things no matter how great or small. Love represents itself in all that you do. You do not have to find it because it lives inside you. There is no need to ask where inside of me is love. Just place yourself in the present moment, let go of all things of the past or future and surrender to the present moment because that is all you really have and that is where true love resides.

In love we can heal all things. We can do all things through love. Love is the light of the almighty power. Love has no resistance. It gains power by being resistance free. As you begin to understand love and its true power you will come to understand it has no barriers. Love is the light of God, the almighty source of all things good and bad.

When you hear me say bad, you may begin to feel unsettled but it is the source of all things, so everything good and bad is included. What you must understand is the bad is not the source, but the free will to choose and follow a path disconnected from the one and only true source of love and light.

To follow the one true source, one must be filled with love. The love and light of the almighty source will guide you and bring you to your destination with very little resistance if you choose to accept it. You do not need to be any kind of special person. When you choose the love and light of the almighty power of God you have chosen the path to victory. Go and fill your heart with love. If anything gets in the way of love let it go. Heal yourself and others through this almighty power and force that is never ending.

Happiness

I am here today to bring you a special message. A message which will bring you much understanding. In this message you will learn what it means to be happy and how to fill your heart with joy so you may always remain in the light. Happiness is not a state from which you ignore. When one is truly happy, life becomes joyful.

So what robs us from this happiness that we seek?

It is thoughts and dissatisfaction with how we perceive our life to be. Our perceptions create our reality and through these perceptions our world is conceived through our eyes. We perceive things to be a certain way and because of this we are dissatisfied with life and ourselves. When you change your perception of how things are supposed to be, you change your reality.

Inside of reality lies the true path to happiness. When you know the truth and perceive a world from love and light, only happiness can reside. Where is your happiness? Happiness is inside of love and light. I am here not to guide you toward your own happiness, because that is done only through your own choosing and how you perceive your world to be. We want you to know that happiness is yours for the asking. You must ask for happiness to be present in your life and when you do you will receive it in accordance to your belief in it.

How do you perceive your world to be in happiness?

This becomes your perception of how you will create your reality and live in the love and light that is all-powerful and good. Joy in life comes from the celebration of what's around you. When you are grateful you are more likely to experience a greater sense of joy. Joy does not come in a bottle like something you can drink. Joy is an experience of life that brings you in connection with the light. When we are joyful we have a much greater capacity to achieve what we want and to experience life in the best way we know without pain and suffering.

How do we be more joyful?

We experience more joy in our life by experiencing more gratitude for what we have around us and from within us. Joy is indescribable when it appears because it comes from within and it cannot be seen. It is an experience we have that elevates who we are. Joy is a higher state of consciousness because it does not bring pain or distraction. We experience joy by placing ourselves in a state of gratitude for everything we know and everything we don't know.

When you can place yourself in a state of gratitude you will begin to notice who you are being and that life is a wonderful experience to be enjoyed. You do not think of the past or the future, you are fully present in the here and now. When we are always looking in the past or the future, we are never fully present. Your job is to remain in the present as much as possible so that you may fully experience the joy life has to offer. Living in the present is the state of being that you most desire. Being in the past or the future is only for determining what you had or what you would like to experience. It is not meant for daily living. All pain and suffering resides in the past and the future. If one lets go of the past or the future all pain and suffering would no longer reside in the body.

What if a person is sick with a disease that is incurable or life-threatening? Can this person be released from their pain and suffering by letting go of the past and future? The answer is no, because more than likely this person's spirit has chosen to have this experience in their lifetime. It is what they wish to learn from the experience that will elevate who they truly are. But there is no definite answer to how a person may experience their life, for though the grace of God all things may be altered.

As you begin your day look to see what is it that you wish to make of it. How will you live this day and what will you do if this day was your last? When we begin our day in this way, we can live our life more fully. No other exercise can bring you closer to understanding your day. Practice this until it becomes a habit for daily living.

In today's world it is not necessary to understand stress because it is all around us. If you understand it, you are aware of it. If you don't understand it, you still know something is there.

Stress is the cause of all discomfort and disease and it tells the body there is something wrong. The body cannot handle large amounts of stress on a daily basis without some kind of side effect.

The only way we can release stress is by doing something about it. If we are experiencing stress of some kind, we must look to see what options are offered to us to release the stress. Stress does not have to be present in life if one is able to see the cause. The cause of stress is released by acceptance of what is occurring and by allowing yourself not to react in a negative way. By doing this we are creating a release for stress to exit our life. If we are to be stress free we are to be accepting to what life has to offer, and if it is not acceptable take the appropriate actions.

Please do not worry. Worry is the part of life that is always incomplete. It is like a duck in the water without the ability to float. You are always in a downward spiral away from the light of the one true source.

If you need to worry about something, worry about who you are being in the moment and ask yourself if that is really you. Make sure you are living in the present moment, not the past or the future. Live life with peace and the understanding that what you believe is what you will achieve. Let no doubt enter your mind and most of all let worry drown itself out of your life for it serves no purpose to lead you to your highest and greatest good.

Inside of love there lies an open heart that is all giving and all loving it does not judge, for its only intention is to give and to love.

Where can we find this open heart?

We find this open heart inside of ourselves. When we focus our intention on only giving and not allowing ourselves to critique or judge anyone or anything, we are beginning to love from the heart.

It's not found without first surrendering to all that's around you and putting yourself in a state of grace filled with the desire to give without concern for what you will receive. You are giving from the heart and through the heart comes true love. The love that is all giving and unconditional. The love that comes through the one true source of all love and light.

So what is it you want to accomplish in this life?

I want to accomplish great things in my life that make a difference and are real to the highest and greatest good of all those I serve. I would like to experience an abundant flow of joy in what I do and in who I am. This joy is always present and always increasing in accordance with who I am being. I would like the world to know I was here and I made a difference, not for myself but for all of humanity. I want to be strong, vibrant and healthy while I am around.

I want to understand the unknown and use the information to serve all of humanity to its highest and greatest good. I would like to be free from all constraints of the past, present and future. I would like to live in abundance this day and always. I would like to experience the peace and love of the eternal Holy Spirit and to always know the truth. I would like to live life without limitations and always know that I am the creator of my world.

Who You Really Are

Today is a day for understanding who you really are. It was given to you before you came to this world. Don't look to another to find out who you really are. No one knows but you because you are unique in your own way. You have many influences and it becomes difficult to see the real you. But the real you is always there and never hiding, just covered up sometimes by all that has come through influence and life.

I know you are saying what is it that influences me or affects my life so that I am not the real me? You see this for yourself when you come to realize that all things are not as they appear to be. When you discover the truth of all that is before you, you begin to see the real you. I am who he is, I am who you are, I am the I am, that is all that needs to be said.

It is not the way of being that interferes with your progress, but who you are being in the moment. If you are feeling sad you are being a certain way that causes it to be so. No one can be sad without sad thoughts. It is not who you are being but it is the thoughts of being sad that make you who you are in that moment. If you are feeling overwhelmed, you are not centered on one task or one desire. You are scattering your mind on too many thoughts causing you to feel uncomfortable.

The multitude of thoughts separates you from who you really are and does not allow you to be in the present moment. I am in the moment when I am here and now. There is no future or past, just now. The present moment allows you to see who you truly are being, the self you were meant to be.

A Special Day

Today is a special day. Although different things may occur on each day, each day should be thought of as special and unique because it brings forth the opportunity for higher spiritual growth. If we bring forth what we know and don't judge what we are doing in the moment, we begin to become free to be who we truly are.

The moment is not the past or the future. It is right now. It has no beginning or ending, it is just now. This concept is not difficult to understand if you allow yourself just to be present and let go of all else that remains. You do not want to live on the street or wander around because you have no means to support yourself in this life. You must keep the essential parts of life in existence in to live and conduct your life appropriately.

It is all in accordance with what you had wished to experience in this lifetime.

So how can all this help you in your current life?

It brings you closer to what your true purpose is meant to be and it separates those things that are not in alignment. In a sense, you are achieving a higher state of consciousness for living the life you were meant to live.

I wish to explain a great many things but all cannot be explained in such a short time. Therefore, let us begin with the first explanation and we will gradually move forward to each subsequent explanation as it comes. In your mind there is no difference between what you think and who you are. But when you do not know yourself there is a great division between the two.

The division exists because the thoughts are not of a real nature. They are illusions the mind created though different experiences in this lifetime. To get back to where you wish to be, you first have to let go of illusions stored in the mind. The release of these illusions is a conscious effort from which you are to begin.

As you begin to let go more and more illusions your mind and thoughts become more unified. They work together as opposed to working against each other.

What can we say about the experience that hasn't been said?

The life of illusions is released for a subtler life in which the mind and thoughts are truly working together. We have spoken about the power of now, that is being in the present. When you consistently bring this state of mind you are allowing the mind to work with the thoughts by not allowing future or past to interfere.

You are beginning to release thoughts that do not serve your highest and greatest good. As you begin more and more each day, you will begin to see an opening of freedom between the mind and thoughts. Those things that caused you to react in the past are no longer in control. The mind and thoughts are more connected to become one unified whole. As you go about your day, notice the progress you are making. Do not allow yourself to become dismayed. When you find yourself at fault for living in the past or future, return to the present moment and begin again. Each time you bring yourself back to the present you will become more aware of the circumstance you are creating. Allow all things to unfold in time and you will receive a great reward.

There is no light without darkness. For you to seek the light you must come out of the darkness. When you have come out, the light will always remain. When you go to bed at night you go to sleep in darkness but upon waking there is light. In very much the same way the spirit leaves the body and comes back, light and darkness of the spiritual nature does as well.

When you have reached a state of consciousness that is aware of this presence of light and darkness you can remain more in the light. But there is no guarantee for the attainment of light for it is only given by God, and as such it is the will of God that you receive it. Don't be concerned whether you will receive it or not. The light is given freely upon expectation of your beliefs. Be at peace and do not worry, you are not alone.

I want to tell you a story. Once there was a king. A mighty and wise king he was. One day the king decided to make all of his subjects worship him as if he were a God. The king did not realize that this would not strengthen his reign, only weaken it. As a result, the king died and all of his subjects and his kingdom died with him because in the eyes of all the people life was not meant to be lived without their God.

So where did this king go wrong?

He took away all of the kingdom's freedom to choose what is right and wrong. The society could not remain in existence because it had lost its free will. All the king had created was lost. In this world, God has given us the free will to choose what we wish to create, whether we believe God is with us or not.

If you are interested in something, you must focus all your mind on it until you have achieved the results you seek. Do not spend time on things you have little interest in. If it does not inspire you or resonate with you such that it feels good to you when you focus on it, don't spend your time on it. Focus on what inspires you and leaves you feeling alive, that is it doesn't drain you when you're doing it. When you focus on what you love, you are most happy and content and very little energy is consumed.

Love is what's missing when the presence of joy is not there. Love from the heart, not the mind, and you will see great joy in your life. Do not worry about things outside yourself, follow what your inner guidance tells you. You do not need to search for anything, for everything is already within you. If you wish to have a new experience that is fine, but it is not necessary to find answers elsewhere. Live your life to the fullest each day. Do not worry what you need to do or what needs to be done. Focus on right now and complete one thing at a time. In this way you will achieve many things in the state of calm peace with freedom and ease.

Love is carried in all things. When you see this you will truly experience the joy and peace of the world. Let your love flow from within you. Love is in and around all things and you will see how God's loving light pours forth through you in everything you do.

I want to tell you a story of two men. One man was born of great wealth and prosperity while the other man was born in absolute poverty. Each man grew up believing there was always something more they were to learn out of life. The prosperous man believed he had to gain more wealth and prosperity. The man of poverty believed he had to gain more love in his heart toward all things he had encountered in his life.

Which man is more prosperous?

The man who seeks more wealth and prosperity or the man who seeks to live his life in total love and gratitude for what he wishes to become. What really matters is how you love and appreciate who you are and all things that come into your experience. This is true happiness and no man or woman could ever ask for more. Let your heart be always filled with love, and when it is not, always stop and ask yourself why? More than likely it is because you are searching or wanting to experience something other than true love. The love that exists only when one seeks it in their life and wishes nothing more than love to remain present from within. When you can truly love yourself and all those around you, you receive the greatest reward anyone could ever ask for — the love and light of the most high.

If you cannot see, where do you go?

Turn from within and quiet the mind so that you can experience the light that is all-powerful and mighty. There is no need for thought, just your presence in total absolute stillness. This is when you will find your understanding and the guidance you long for.

I wish to give you these three points.

First, do not leave your schedule open for idleness. Let your schedule focus on the value you are to create in this world. Let go of all attachments when you are working and seek only the value you wish to give from your heart. Do not be disappointed when you do not see things going in the way you had expected. Just look for the lesson to be learned. Allow all things to unfold as they may through peace, calmness and, most importantly, love. Second, as you begin this process don't worry about doing things right or wrong, have no judgment. Everything flows from the heart and when you allow it to come through you will know the outcome is for you. Third, there is no light in darkness. When darkness comes over you, you must seek the light. To speak from the heart, you must always come from the love and light of the Holy Spirit.

These are the messages we have for you and we hope that you take them into consideration as you go about your day, living life to your highest and greatest good.

Appreciate Where You Are Now

Do not be disappointed with yourself. All things in life take time. Appreciate where you are now and know that you will get to where you want to go. It is all a matter of intention, and when you intend to do something you will always get there as long as you stay committed to the intention. Let your heart be at peace and your mind be at ease. There is no need for worry or doubt. Just enjoy where you are right now and know you will get to where you want to go. There is nothing you are doing that will get you there faster than you are already going, so just allow the process to unfold.

Today is a day for understanding. When you are confused about something, the way to remedy the problem is to be quiet and still. No answers will come to you if your mind is aloud with thoughts rambling on and on. Let your mind be still and quiet and when you are at peace the answers will start to come.

Confusion can no longer exist when the mind is quiet and still. It has nothing to thrive on when the mind is quiet. As a result, the mind is able to receive understanding because it is no longer distracted. When this is the case many questions can be answered. "I no longer wish to be in the presence of mind distractions" should be your mantra. It is the key to always maintaining a clear focus and direction.

Where do I go from here?

From here you go to the next step, which is always right in front of you. Never try to skip steps and jump ahead because when you do, it interferes with the flow of momentum. One step at a time is all you need to take. As you proceed from one step to the next you will build upon what you know and achieve the highest and greatest results.

Love is the most important aspect to keep in your life. Do not worry about anything except when there is an absence of love in your heart. This absence of love causes you to doubt yourself and give in to that which is not for you. Despair is not what life is meant to be. The absence of love can bring you to places you do not want to go. In love all things are possible because you are filled with the Holy Spirit of light and love. There is peace from within not despair.

As you begin to love life you begin to see the presence of love in all things. When the presence of love shows itself, you are in a state where love is your guiding principle. All we have to say is begin with love in your heart and let it manifest itself in all that you do. When the moments come where you feel in your heart the absence of love, rekindle this light so that it may once again shine in your heart, the love and light of the Holy Spirit.

We say Holy Spirit to mean of the highest and greatest good. This love and light is what connects you to all that is, was and ever shall be. It is all empowering love. I love you, why do you worry so much? Just be present in the here and now and enjoy the experience. There is nothing you need to do but see the present moment of now. If you let go of all you know and have learned and allow yourself to be in this moment of now, you will see what you are searching for. The peace and love of now is all that matters. Love lights the way to true happiness.

If you want to go far, don't worry about the distance you must travel. Take one step at a time until you get there. There is no need for worry or to wonder when you will arrive, just enjoy the experience of the journey. If you need to stop to rest from time to time, this is OK, too. There is no rush as long as you have set an intention for where you want to go. You will always get there in the right time.

Remember it is not how far you go in life that's important, but the journey from one place to the next. When there is no worry or rush you remain in the state of love and light from which you came.

In you is all the potential you ever wanted, when you allow it to come out. There is no need for wondering how, just allow it and it will be. This is what most people call faith or belief, without it you are always living in limitation. When you believe in what you would like to experience, know that it has already been given to you. If it is meant for you it is just a matter of time until it manifests itself into reality. What your mind conceives and believes will become your reality.

All it takes is believing in what you would like to experience. There is no need to worry how it will happen because once you believe, the opportunities and experiences will start to happen automatically. This is called manifesting from the mind.

What brings you to this state of being?

All things are not as they appear? If you let go of what disturbs you, you begin to see what is in your way. It is an illusion. When you are living in an illusion you are living in a state of disconnect from what is real and true. The truth does not exist within you until you are willing to let go of false perceptions and enter into the love and light of the Holy Spirit that is whole complete and true. In this way you are complete and living life as it was meant to be, in the love and light of the most high.

False pride will always send you in misguided directions. Until you seek to understand who you are being you will not remain in the present moment. You will be misguided with thoughts of the past or future, but never really being here right now. When you are not in the moment of now you are traveling in misguided directions and your path of understanding will always be unclear. Once again, this is the moment to let go of the past or future and return to the present moment of now where all love and light begins and never ends.

It is time to understand what is missing and what is not missing. If you look at your life you can clearly see what is missing because you feel that you can't have it or don't believe it can be yours. But there is something else that needs to be looked at and that is what you already have. You see you already have everything you need. You think there is something missing, but you are all whole and complete. God would not have it any other way.

So why are you so displeased with yourself?

You have come to believe there is something missing and without it you are incomplete. But the only thing you need is love because all things come from love. That is the love and peace that comes from your heart. You do not need to look anywhere else but there in the space of love in the heart. Love from the heart is all that really matters, it brings you joy and peace and it brings you what you most would like to experience in this life.

Love from the heart is the guiding light that brings you where you truly wish to go. There is no need to search for anything because it is all right from the heart. All we have to do is believe in this love from the heart and experience the blessings that manifest themselves as your love flows from within. It is a great mistake to be misguided by those who only wish to take from you what you already have. They make you think there is something missing. But if you believe and trust in the love of the heart nothing can take it away except for your own thinking and choosing. You are now ready to live with love from the heart, as you were always meant to be.

Keep this love always flowing in your heart and you will always know that you are whole and complete as life was meant to be. Love is here today, it is here tomorrow, and all that is needed is to be connected to it through the simple surrounding of all attachments. Attachments are those things that prevent you from experiencing love. If we are to advance in life, we must free ourselves from any attachments that prevent us from experiencing the true love and light of the Holy Spirit. It is not in the way you live your life that matters. It is who you have become and what you have learned from this experience. All that really matters is how much you loved yourself and others as yourself. In what context did you bring this love to the world? Love is kind, love is giving, love is understanding, love is patient, love does not judge. It seeks to understand and allows that which is in its path to flow to the highest and greatest good.

Can I know love if I don't feel love?

Love is all around you, it is always there, you do not feel love because you are not present or receptive to its existence. Love does not require anything from you, it is always available to you whenever you wish to receive it.

What stops us from being present to love?

What's stopping you from the presence of love is you and your desire to have it now. If you are not experiencing love now, you are not choosing it now. Love does not exist to serve you or to ask for rewards if you are good. It just is and always was and ever shall be. It is your decision to choose it in any moment, for only love can bring light upon darkness, which could never prevail in the contest of love and light.

In conclusion, there is love in all things and it is always and forever present without any expectations. Love is the all-encompassing source of light that leads the way to joy, peace and happiness.

I want to tell you a story. This story is not about anyone you know. It is about what you don't know. You can only see and understand what you know, and what you don't know is unseen or unavailable to you. The things that you don't know are available to you once you are able to let go of the past and begin to see them in a different way. "I don't know what I don't know" is a frequent statement to keep in mind, because it allows you to explore what is unseen in the present moment.

Being present to what is happening in the now we are able to explore what we don't know. It can come to us without any effort or understanding. We are what we know and what we don't know remains unseen. To see what we don't know we must begin to realize there is more to see than what we know. It is through a transformation in our perceptions that we see what we'd never seen before. It brings us to a new stage of reality that we didn't know existed, the moment our perception changed.

If you do not see what is in front of you, you do not see where you are going. It is a matter of choice to move in one direction or another. But when you begin to see in front of you, you see where you are going.

Why are we so upset sometimes over little or nothing at all?

We are upset because we have not learned to let go of things that take away from us in some way, but in reality there is nothing that can take anything away from you and there is no reason for anger or despair. We are what we create, and we create the context in which despair will exist.

The survival of any meaning we create for ourselves depends on us alone. We decide to become angry because we create a meaning in which the context for anger can exist. So if we can create the context for anger we can also create the context for love and peace. When we choose, we are truly in control of our life and the circumstances that may unfold.

There is no peace if you do not choose peace. Reacting to a cause without choosing is like living a life that controls you without your permission. When you react to a cause you are giving yourself permission to lose control and be misguided for nothing good can come out of anger, hatred or darkness. It rules you and controls you without giving you what you most long for in life, the peace and love of joy that makes life so worth living.

If you cannot see this, it is because you are choosing to be right about something you believe is true. You may have created a story about it and have all the evidence in the world to prove you are right. But once again, you are wrong, because the love and light of the Holy Spirit cannot exist in your judgments of right and wrong. It can only supply that from which it is, the love and light of the most high and powerful.

If you choose not to accept it you are choosing darkness over light, because you want to be right about something you perceive to be true. But the real truth is only in love and light and anything that takes away from this love — no matter how right it may seem — is a lie to deceive you from the truth. The truth is there is no right or wrong. In love and light there is only love and to choose anything other than this is to choose a life of darkness.

All is well. In you I am, in me I am, we are all one. There is no separation, we are connected. Now stop for a moment and think about what you truly want. It does not make sense to think about things you do not want because you can never attract what you want until you have become focused.

There are no easy or hard ways of doing this manifesting. You just focus on what you want until it becomes your reality. There is no resistance or doubt, just a knowingness it is on its way. Patience is key and what you must learn along the way for true growth and development. The expansion of self is part of that experience. Live from within yourself and allow what there is to be learned to come to you, and you will live the life you were meant to live.

There needs to be no further explanation except that in all you do always choose the love and light of the Holy Spirit to exist in your heart, no matter how right you may feel about something. Choosing love whenever you're faced with a choice is the only way for you to live a life in love and peace to your highest and greatest good.

Through Love and Light

Inside every diamond is a circle of light that protrudes from the inside out. It is not from the outside that light comes through, but from the inside. As you are living your life notice where your thoughts are coming from — the outside or the inside. If they come from inside you will feel a sense of love and comfort. The thoughts from the inside come from love and light and are only meant for your highest and greatest good. Allow yourself to take notice of these thoughts and they will take you toward higher heights of development. It is through love and light that you reach your point of destiny. If there is to be light in anything there needs to be love.

Love does not exist without the light and so love and light are inseparable, one cannot exist without the other.

What's in your mind is not real if it does not serve you to your highest and greatest good. Love is real, it is all that matters. When love is in the heart the mind is no longer controlled by what is not real. But it is when the mind takes over and does not allow love to be present in the heart. That's when we see a separation.

If we are to be free we are to surround ourselves with love that comes from the heart. Not love in the physical sense of pleasure and procreation, but love that leads you to the truth because it has no judgments or demands. It only is love in its purest sense. Every time love leaves your heart you are being misguided by things not in alignment with your highest and greatest good.

So where is the love when we are angry?

It is always there. It is only through our choosing that it can exist. We are attached to what is not real, though we may perceive it to be real. The only thing that is real is love and that is the love and light of the most high. If we are to receive it, we must be open to accepting love in our hearts and rejecting all that is not in alignment with love, no matter how real or right it may seem. Choosing love is what life is truly all about. When we are present to this love in our hearts we experience life as it was meant to be, releasing all tension, anger, fear, and hatred for an all-consuming sense of joy and satisfaction.

Today is a beautiful day as all days should be. In looking at your day it is all a matter of perception, and when you want to create a world that works for you it is key to be aware of what perceptions you are creating and what perceptions you are holding on to that no longer serve you. You begin to see everything you create and how you are creating your world.

Wow! You may say how can I create my world when things seem to just happen and I have no control over them? This is not true because you have control over all things you create. As you create so shall it be. We are creating in every moment and our thoughts create our reality. When we change our thoughts we change our reality, it is just that simple.

How do we change our thoughts?

We change our thoughts by choosing to think about what we truly want to create. When we are focused and aware of what we are creating we are more in control of our reality. I say more because sometimes we think we are fully aware when in reality we are not. So awareness is a key component in creating your reality and being in control of it. It does not happen overnight, it takes practice and persistent determination to let go of all that is stopping you from living the life you were meant to live.

We were all meant to live a life we love. But it is through our experiences that our true reality turns in to a world of entanglement. We are trapped in our own webs of deception and illusion and until we can realize the truth of the matter, we will continue to do so without awareness of what we are creating. We are in a trap and the trap is ourselves and what we perceive to be our world. But there can only be one world and that is the world of peace, love and joy in which we live a life without judgment and exist in all-encompassing love and peace.

The desire to live in this kind of world can only be manifested by focusing on what is most important, the love and light of what is and what always was — the love and light of peace and love. You may say how can I feel peace and love when I am so angry and unable to think peaceful thoughts? It is your ability to handle, do anything you choose to do from your own free will and determination. You have to stop in the moment and realize where you are and who you are being. Once you take hold of this you are beginning to take control over your world and your life. We are what we intend to be. You are no longer a prisoner of a world without control, you are free to choose.

When I say you are now free to choose it is through your self-determinism. No one is telling you what to do, it is all coming from you and what you intend to create and that is the world around you in peace, love, happiness and joy. There can be no greater delight.

We are delighted to know you are at peace with your loved ones. Please do not make this a cause for distraction of who you are. You are love and love is all around you. It is not that you are at peace with your loved ones but that you are connected to this eternal source of love. Love does not exist outside of yourself, it is from within that you experience this sensation. When we say sensation we mean sensation, for there is nothing greater one can experience than love. There is no need for searching to find love.

Love exists here and now and doesn't need to be found. As we go through life we become thwarted from what we truly love and what we truly experience as joy. The time has come for us to remain present in the here and now and to reside in it so that we may shine bright like a diamond.

Healing From Love

I need to know what ails you in order for you to be healed. In healing there is no need. There is a letting go of what no longer serves the body. So healing is not a need it is a release, a release of those things that came to us but are no longer serving us to our highest and greatest good.

Releasing is letting go of what we've become attached to. We feel it is right to hold on because otherwise we would be treated unfairly or not receive the justice we deserve. But all is given to those who are willing to place love in their hearts above all things. Love is the highest form of healing and it is only when we let go of all that we are attached to that we can fully experience love.

Experiencing love is not a feeling that justice has been served. It is surrendering all things past and present for an all-consuming light that only knows love. We will move quickly in this process of love because when this light surrounds you, you are in a state of invincibility and nothing is in your way but pure love.

In love all things are possible and you do not have to fear life, because you know that the way to true peace and happiness is love. Surround yourself in love and begin to let go of all attachments that have interfered with experiencing true love and light. This is a state of experience that you were born to live in this lifetime.

What is it in life that you want?

Is it peace and love or is it riches and fame? Don't you know you can have anything you want in life just by asking? So what are you asking for? Creating a vision on things and experiences is the most powerful tool you can use to create what you want in life. Just write out your life story and speak it into reality.

Once you can clearly see your vision you won't have to wait long before it arrives. Once you can see and know what you want all the other steps will begin to fall in place without much effort on your part. It is only when you begin to resist life that things become difficult. Let go of all resistance and just allow things to flow. Write your story on a daily basis. It is much easier to write a story and believe it than it is to write a list of items that seem to overwhelm you. It is in the thinking and doubting that resistance will take place.

Surely you cannot achieve greatness if you believe you can't. But if it is a story that you have written, you are the creator and who's to say it's not possible?

There is no point debating the topic. If you wish to manifest what you want in life, just become the author of your life and write and believe what you say as the truth. In this way all things become possible in line with your belief and what you wish to experience. Remember this is in accordance with your life and your belief. You cannot become the author of someone else's life, that is for them to create.

How should I focus my time?

Focus your time on things you love doing and do them well. This does not mean you should ignore everything else that needs to be done to keep your life in order. We are speaking of the time that's yours when there is nothing to do but choose how to spend it. Stay focused on what's important but do not be misguided by distractions that lead you in a different direction. A project cannot be completed if you start another one and focus your attention elsewhere. Focus on one project at a time and if you feel you are getting bored take a break but do not search for something else to do.

Things that are meant to do on a daily basis, like play a musical instrument or exercise, are good as time away from your project. Remember your project is your primary concern and all other actions are secondary regarding work, not family or friends. Focus your attention on one project at a time and allow time for that project to be completed before starting anything else.

What if I am not making any progress on my current project?

Clearing away things that do not support the current project is a high priority. Also, creating a not-doing-now project list is also desirable because it will help you to avoid becoming distracted and losing focus on the original project. You don't want to start a new project until you have received results and completed the project you started. The fewer incompletes you have the more power and inspiration you will have to complete what you are working on.

It's about becoming clear on your main focus and how you will support that focus with the intention of completing each action you've started. The trap is starting other smaller projects that begin to distract you and diminish your focus on what you started out to do. You must decide on what comes first and decide on the other areas you would like to include in your daily work schedule. The key here is not to waste time.

To not waste time you must know what you are spending time on. If it is your project, designate the time you spend on it. If it is something else, also designate time for it, but remember not to do too much or you will accomplish very little. It is your intention that will help you to see what needs to be done. In everything you do, consider what value it is creating and is the time spent worth the effort. In this, you will see what best to do.

Are there any daily activities I should be doing?

Daily activities are what bring you the highest reward. When things are done consistently you will have mastered them to the highest level. Do what you most desire to achieve in your life experience. Do it well and you will achieve the full benefits of what it has to offer.

What is Holding You Back?

There is nothing holding you back except for constraints you put on yourself. You believe something is not possible and you doubt yourself and come to believe you are not capable. But in reality you are capable of all things you set your mind to do. The only obstacles are your own thoughts and judgments telling you that you're not capable of accomplishing the task.

As a result, you begin to search outside yourself to find the answers for which you're searching. There is no reason to do this because you already have the answers inside you. Your doubts and disbelief are taking you on a wild goose chase. They are prompting you to go in all directions, leading you nowhere.

The only course of action for believing in one's self is to set an intention and allow it to happen. Your intention will begin to manifest itself in many ways. All you have to do is be open and receptive to guidance and inspiration toward the desired outcome.

How Do We Become Clear as to
Understanding What We Truly Desire?

The best way to become clear is to decide on what you don't want and create an intention for what is desired. Everything is accomplished in time with inspired action and guidance from within. It becomes a great joy to know all you have to do is stop, look and listen to what is already been given to you and proceed from there.

How Can I Lead A More Rewarding Life?

Do not worry! Worry is the downfall of all happiness. It leads to a place of despair. Worry is a disguise for confusion or doubt. It does not believe in what is real and possible. Leading a good life requires belief in yourself and not thinking in terms of outcome, but in the present moment. I don't wish to lead you to despair but to the present moment. To live in the present is to live life with joy, and there can be no greater reward than to live a joyful life.

How Do We Live in the Present Moment?

You live in the present by focusing attention on what's happening right now. There are no thoughts of the past or the future, you're just being here right now, observing and appreciating what is taking place.

What if you observe something that is not good?

It is your choice to do something about it or not. But you do not leave the present moment, you remain calm and take action/not take action without any reaction to what's taking place.

There is really no doubt. You seek answers but you already know them. You are not trusting yourself. This is doubting what you already know, which leads to nowhere because you repeat the same cycle of searching because you don't understand it. There is no need for perfection here. When you learn something know you know it, and if you want to review it do so, but move on to something else. When you view the same picture over and over, the image does not change. To change the picture, you must be able to change your vision.

It doesn't matter where you are or who you are being, God is always with you. If we are to understand what this means, we are to understand ourselves and each and every moment we breathe. I am, that which I am is me. If we can hold on to who we truly are, we can live the lives we were meant to live in peace love and joy.

What Does it Mean to Experience Love?

Love is the direct communication with all that is, ever was and ever shall be. It is the light of the most high that gleams down on us. There is nothing missing in life. Everything you need you already have. It is the moment when you believe you don't have something that everything seems to change, making you believe there is something missing. But there is never anything missing, only your perception of what's real and true for you.

If we believe in a greater consciousness we need to believe we are a part of what we know to be true. If we are part of the higher consciousness most people in the world call God, we believe if we are a part of God we have all we need. As we begin to grow away from this belief, we separate ourselves from God. We no longer feel part of this greater and higher consciousness. Life leads to despair and disbelief. We are no longer able to access things we are capable of having because our needs are clouded with disbelief.

All you would like to experience is yours for the asking. You are part of a higher consciousness that brings into light everything you have and ever wanted. If I am not connected to the source of all abundance, I know I am living in disbelief and there can be no joy or real value in this kind of thinking.

Today is not like any other day because each day is special in its own way. Take, for example, the birds in the air. Each bird flies in its own space yet they are together. The individual space is unique and belongs only to the bird that occupies it. Like the birds, we are occupying a space in which we choose to fly in any direction we want. It is the sense of knowing we are individuals, but not separate from the flock.

There is emptiness inside of me and I don't know why it is there. How do I find the cause of what is troubling me now?

Why are you so unhappy? Is it because you refuse to learn from experience and you create a story so you can justify it being the truth for you? In reality it is all a lie that you created because you were unwilling to see the truth. No one is capable of seeing the truth if they don't want to learn from life experiences. What we learn in this life is to expand the essence of who we are. When we truly know who we are we no longer justify our experiences through stories that are not true.

Our experiences should always remain in the present that is the very moment of now. If you are living your experience from the past or the future, you are not living in truth because everything is a judgment of the past or future. Frustration is a sign of things you feel are not working the way you feel they should. But remember, everything is a lesson. So when something goes in a different direction than you thought, it should look not for what is wrong but the lesson to be learned.

Today is a day for understanding. When we look into who we truly are we begin to see we are all the same and the only things that make us different is thoughts and messages that have gone into our heads. We may look different in a sense of structure but that is not who we truly are. The outer body is merely a shell that contains who we truly are and if we were to be put into another body nothing would change. We would remain the same. So why are we so concerned with the body when that is not who we truly are? It is from within the body that we exist. We do not live outside of the body until we leave its remains here on this planet.

I do not understand what's so difficult to see when you know you are not of this body. If you are not of this body, to exist is to live in the body for a period of time.

When this time is up and we no longer live in the body, our existence still remains. We go on living in another existence beyond our current understanding. As we become aware of this new existence, we are challenged to choose what types of experiences we would like to have. These are created from our choices and put into motion for us to experience as we wish for the development and expansion of who we are.

There is no decision made by anyone but you. Everything decided has been decided out of your own choices and decisions. It may sound unusual for you to have made all choices you wish to experience, but this is what is so and how you come to a greater expansion of who you are and have become.

Today is all that exists. Yesterday is gone and tomorrow is yet to come. Be here right now and let go of the past and live in the present. The present is the only place true joy can be found. I am here right now because I am fully present to this moment and nothing more. Life brings me joy in the moment.

The Life I Want To Live

I am free to choose the life I want to live. I choose the present moment of now. If something is bothering me or disturbing me, I look to see where it is coming from and I allow myself to release that which is not for my highest and greatest good. Amen, I am at peace. Approach all things with love. Let it be the source from which you come and let the light of the most Holy Spirit shine upon you through this love and light.

Today is a day like no other. It is a day to celebrate a new life, for with each day a new life begins. We do not mean in the process of birth but from within your own life. Each day we begin a new life with new experiences that teach us lessons for expansion and growth. We are born again to something new each day that expands our understanding and wisdom. The only times we are not learning is when we expand our thoughts into false realities that do not serve to our highest and greatest good.

You are just beginning to understand the process for your journey to manifest itself. It is only a matter of time until you have become secure in what you are doing, so that it brings you great joy and happiness. Let there be light upon everything you do and let this be your point of no return.

So here we are at the end of a completion of something we know is just the beginning. Now where do we go from here? It is important to remember that there is nowhere to go but the here and now. The present moment is all you need to know and from this point you will know your next step.

Every step is just a means of expanding and growing to your highest and greatest good. With love and joy, may the peace of the most holy light shine upon you each and every day in the present moment of now.

With Love,
Michael F Canciglia

Printed in the United States
By Bookmasters